Rise Of The Courageous Leader

Rise Of The Courageous Leader

Ally Nitschke

Published by Ally Nitschke

First published in 2022 in Australia

Copyright © Ally Nitschke

www.madeformore.com.au

Typeset, printed and bound in Australia by BookPOD

ISBN: 978-0-6455001-0-3 (pbk)
ISBN: 978-0-6455001-1-0 (ebook)

NATIONAL
LIBRARY
OF AUSTRALIA

A catalogue record for this
book is available from the
National Library of Australia

Acknowledgements

This book has been a labour of love. After two complete re-writes a couple of near 'throw the whole lot in the bin' moments and a lot of late nights and early mornings I have a lot of people to thank.

Firstly my incredible coach, Jane Anderson who has gently encouraged me to write this book and share my expertise with the world. It's very important to have a cheer leader in your corner. I'm very lucky to have a world-class in mine.

My very clever, and very patient editor Kristen Lowery who is a word genius! Thank you for making me sound cleverer than I am, and finessing my words. Having you on the team is a dream come true.

My incredible team, Phuntsho, Nim and Tashi who have worked tirelessly behind the scenes to keep me on track and make everything look beautiful on the outside.

My clients, past, present and future who are continuing to collectively lift the leadership experience and lead with Courage for themselves, their team and their organisations. Also a special thanks to those who ordered and supported this book in it's early stages.

Last and certainly not least, my husband and tiny people who have created space, been quiet when I've been concentrating, found their own snacks when I've been on a writing spree and have supported me to no end in both business and the writing of this book.

To my sunshine; Max, Harvey, Theo and Eddy.
May you grow up in a world that's full of courage
and kindness. The world needs more of you!

Contents

How to use this book

This book is intended to be used as a handbook for leaders, helping you to navigate your leadership journey.

Each chapter of this book focuses on a key competency for courageous leadership™ at the end of each chapter you'll see a page on 'Flexing your Courageous Leader™ muscle (competency).

I'd encourage you to use those pages to start looking at what's working, what's not and what your next step is.

As you go through each competency, I'd encourage you to make your own notes to further integrate your learnings and build your own courageous leadership™ processes, identity and playbook.

Additional resources can be downloaded from www.madeformore.com. au/resources

Introduction

For many years I was a professional dancer in Adelaide. In fact, I spent my entire life in a studio, rehearsing or on a stage. Then arts industry funding was cut in South Australia, and it wasn't too long before I found my hopes and dreams lost. Everything that I had worked for to become a *prima* ballerina was literally swept out from under my feet, leaving me rudderless and jobless. I had to find a new career.

I grew up in a country town. Of course, it's not country anymore, but 15 years ago we still had a central main street, and many of the people that worked in the shops were friends and acquaintances. One Friday I was walking down the main street and as I walked past my local Credit Union, I had a sudden feeling that it might be a great place to work. So, I decided to pop in and see if they would hire me. After all, I'd been banking there for over 18 years. Propelled by that inspiration, I walked into the foyer and simply said, 'Hey, can I have a job?' By Monday, I began as an employee.

Recruiters and HR people know that this likely wouldn't happen today, but 15 years ago it was still something that happened occasionally, particularly in smaller towns. And interestingly, I've found that this sudden burst of inspiration is usually the way that we find something that we love and that we tend to be quite good at it. And once we find that thing, we get invested and we start looking for more opportunities.

The dancing industry was very competitive. We were always competing, always pushing ourselves to the max to reach the next level, physically, emotionally, mentally and creatively. This competitiveness is a thriving part of the banking environment as well. And I loved every minute of it.

Before too long, I was promoted and then promoted again. It was pretty fun. And then I was handed the keys to open up my very own office right in the heart of the city. I got to hand-select my dream team—the people that I wanted to work with and that I knew could perform exceptionally. And because of that I was able to build a really high-performing, dynamic team.

This was a really great time in my career. But of course, nothing lasts forever, and about 10 years ago, we were hit with the global financial crisis. Banking and finance was not a great place to be working at that particular time and eventually we were disbanded, and the office was closed. My team, who were fantastic, were promoted to other areas. And I found myself sent to 'fix a toxic environment' at another office.

The first day in my new role I walked into the office, and it felt like walking into a literal wall of 14 women. They hated their jobs. They hated each other. They hated their boss. And, as you can imagine, they especially hated me—a super optimistic person who had suddenly appeared to sort them out.

This was my baptism of fire when it came to leadership. I learned very quickly that I'd been thrown into the deep end and I either needed to learn to swim or I was going to sink fast. I think that I had sunk quite a few times.

But one of the best parts of this role was that I got to have a vast number of courageous conversations with each and every one of those 14 women. And over the next 18 months we were able to collaboratively turn that team around.

Of course, if you've been on either the giving or receiving end of a courageous conversation, you'll know that it's pretty tiring. And I was ready for a bit of a break. So, I decided on another career change. And this one might have been my hardest (but best role ever)—having four babies, all boys, in five years.

I've learned a lot from each of my careers. And my career as a mum was no different. From my darling three, four, six and eight-year-old children, I've learned the hugely important lessons that all adults have the same emotions, issues and meltdowns as children. And we still have the same difficulties using our words. The only difference is that we're much better at hiding it as adults.

In this book we're tackling this process of using our words through courageous conversations. In my work today I get to collaborate with leaders all around Adelaide, Australia and even the world. And this is something that I speak about quite a bit. How to be a courageous leader, capable of courageous conversations with ourselves and our teams.

While this book is very much workplace related, a lot of that we will deal with here can be used to great effect in our personal lives as well.

Why is Courageous Leadership™ important

'I do not believe you can do today's
job with yesterday's methods
and be in business tomorrow.'

—Nelson Jackson

In a time of texting, tweeting and tagging, now more than ever people are looking for connection. And they are looking to their leaders for that connection.

Because of this we're seeing a new style of leadership emerge. There's a move away from traditional leadership and a view that it simply doesn't work anymore. That it's not enough. And in the last 12 months, we've seen the rate of change accelerate beyond what we thought possible.

What we want and need today are resilient leaders. Leaders who are bold, who can make decisions and who are willing to experiment, test and learn the best ways to lead in our changing environments. But most importantly, we want leaders that have compassion for themselves and for their people.

The root of the word for courage is cor – the Latin word for heart. In its earlier form courage mean "to speak one's mind by telling all one's heart. The future of leadership needs more heart.

What we need are Courageous Leaders™

Courageous leaders embody innovative leadership that fosters creativity, empathy and connection. With a rapidly changing environment and continually competing priorities, leaders today need to step up to adopt these leadership traits. Unfortunately, it's yet to happen. And many human resource managers and general managers' report that while their leaders have great business acumen, they're still missing these important soft skills.

This means that putting out people management fires and having the tough conversations that comes with leadership are often escalated to HR or higher management rather than being efficiently and conscientiously handled within teams.

	ACTIVITY	FOCUS	INFLUENCE
7	Courageous	Impact	100%
6	Confident	Conviction	75%
5	Coasting	Ownership	50%
4	Clear	Plan	20%
3	Frazzled	Delegate	10%
2	Floundering	Clarity	-10%
1	Frozen	Action	-20%

HR managers and GMs are already struggling with time and resources. Having to lead and manage leaders or a leader's people, adds another layer that slows down an organisation's ability to react to emergencies and current priorities and take the right steps at the right time.

HR managers and GMs are continually thinking about the well-being and safety of their workforce while trying to rapidly upskill their people and plan strategically. Being the workplace moderator is not high on the priority list. Nor should it be. This should rightly be in the wheelhouse of the leader.

Following the above model, these are the stages we see leaders go through.

1. Frozen

Leaders at this level are a bit like a deer in headlights. They are usually newly appointed leaders and are perhaps a little overwhelmed with what lies ahead. They may have a large and never-ending to-do list, or are unsure as to what tasks they need to undertake as part of their role. Leaders that are at this level need to focus on Action. Taking action, and action will build that momentum for them to get going. They really need to focus on the next step they're going to take rather than how to climb the entire mountain.

2. Floundering

Leaders at this level are playing a game of 'whack-a-mole'. They are constantly putting out fires, whether they're real or perceived. These leaders also often feel like their leadership journey is 'hard work'. They haven't yet adapted or developed their own leadership style. They may be trying to mimic something they've seen in the past, but it's not working for them. Leaders are this level need to focus on Clarity. The clarity piece in leadership is so important. I often say leaders need to slow down (and plan and think) to speed up (lead and execute). Leaders at this level need to focus on their leadership identity and blueprint and really take a step back to see what their big vision is all about.

3. Frazzled

Leaders at this level are usually a flurry of activity. They're overworked and working long hours, they will often come across as 'busy'. Sometimes, they're busier than they are productive. They are also often doing a lot of work that isn't necessarily in their zone of genius. Leaders at this level need to focus on Delegation. Looking at who in their team can take on some of the tasks that are either taking up a lot of time or taking them away from the more important strategic planning and thinking.

Mastering delegation is a skill every leader learns over time. I cover more on delegation in chapter 5 – Communication.

4. Clear

Leaders at this level have taken the time and discipline to really get to know themselves and have developed a clear vision of what type of leader they want to be. Leaders at this level need to focus on Ownership. Now that they are clear on what type of leader they want to be, they need to take personal responsibility for the next steps. Planning their goals, being accountable to themselves and to others. Driving their own learning and advancement here is really important to build momentum.

5. Coasting

Leaders at this level are cruising, they're no longer frantic. However they're not yet making an impact or influencing those around them. These leaders need to develop and action plan, and then plan how they're going to execute it.

6. Confident

Leaders are this level are often quite confident, they're building their strategic alignment and focusing on leading change within their team and across the organisation. Perhaps they've been in their role for a while, and have some runs on the board. Leaders at this level are usually looking to take the next step in their leadership journey, or are looking to make a bigger impact. Leaders are this level need to focus on Conviction. This means keeping promises to themselves and holding an unwavering belief in what they have to do and who they have to be next

7. Courageous

Leaders at this level are ready to focus on what their impact is going to be, and what legacy they're going to leave behind. They're displaying the 10Cs of Courage in every aspect of their work life. They have a reputation for being a brilliant leader, they're also humble enough to know that leadership is a lifelong journey and their next focus needs to be on being Candid. This means building relationships around them and across the organisation and industry.

At the end of the day, we don't need more hours. We need better leaders. Leaders who can take the reins. Leaders who can step up and lead their teams. Leaders that can have those tough, courageous conversations while maintaining empathy and care.

The people part of business

Certainty in today's fast paced and ever-changing world relies on the ability to adapt and change just as quickly. As leaders we need to be able to respond rather than react. We need to resolve what didn't work and push forward towards a new way of working that does work well.

The weight of responsibility to make sure everyone is safe, retain staff, manage sick and stress leave, not to mention handle the fallout of mental health in the next 12 months and beyond, falls solely on human resources and executives. It's no wonder we're steering directly toward burnout.

But the people part of our business is vital. We must get this right in order to be effective leaders over the long haul. And this book will help you to find the way forward, to be able to lead your people and your teams with empathy, care, innovation and, most importantly, courage.

Let's dive in!

Part 1

Self-Aware (Lead Yourself)

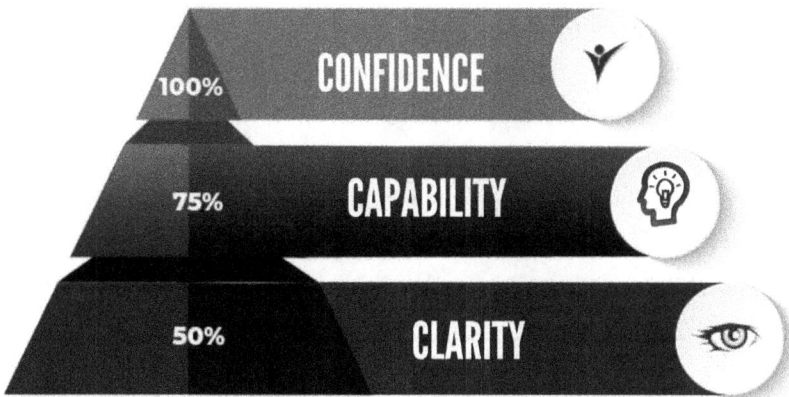

Made For More definition: For leaders to be able to lead a team, first they need to be able to lead themselves, for this to happen they need self-awareness and resilience.

"A leader is ruthlessly self-aware."

—Unknown

For leaders to be able to lead a team, first they need to be able to lead themselves. For this to happen they need self-awareness and resilience.

In 2010 I was fortunate enough to trek the Himalayas. This was a philanthropic expedition to raise funds for some much-needed toilets in the north-western rural region of Chamba Valley.

The purpose for our trek was very much a simple solution to a complex problem. What would happen is that the villagers that lived 'up the hill' would do their business, and when rainfall came, the water would wash their excrement down the hill and into the natural flowing water source that was the source of water for villagers who were further down the hill. With no way to filter the water directly from the source many of the villagers were becoming quite sick. The only way, as they say, was up.

In the lead up to our trip there were multiple fund-raising events to raise funds to build toilets. This money was provided to the villagers to obtain the materials and skills they needed to build the toilets. The reason for our trek then was not to build the toilets themselves. But to meet the village elder who was charged with building the toilets and view the toilets in construction.

We trekked uphill, through the Himalayas for four days before we saw anything that resembled a toilet. But when we finally arrived at a small village on the fifth day to see one of these toilets, we were amazed by the incredible craftsmanship that had gone into this work.

Under the strong leadership of the village elder, the villagers had learned the skills they needed in order to build modern working toilets. They had sourced and purchased the right equipment and products. And they had worked conscientiously and collaboratively to get the job underway. The results were outstanding. And the entire village was benefitting from the strength of this single leader and this single team.

The outcomes for your own team might not be as physically vital as the outcomes for these rural villagers. But you can certainly get equally fantastic results in your own sphere. When teams and leaders work together and have a singular focus and goal, and when they can see the benefits and outcomes that they can achieve together, they are motivated to do the job and do it well. But to get our teams there, we have to become self-aware as leaders. We need to be able to lead ourselves and do it well. This includes:

- Clarity—having a clear vision on where you are and where you want to be.
- Capability—understanding your abilities, what you're capable of and great at and the awareness of the areas that you need support in.
- Confidence—having the ability to show your passion for your beliefs and values as well as consistent and predictable behaviour.

Chapter 1

Clarity

Made For More definition: Clarity is having a clear vision on where you are now and where you want to be. It allows you to construct a compelling future for yourself.

> 'Clarity is the preoccupation of the effective leader. If you do nothing else as a leader, be clear.'
>
> —Marcus Buckingham

Clarity is Your Leadership Foundation

Clarity is the foundational piece for all leaders. Without clarity there is no direction.

Yet, clarity is often the most overlooked piece for leaders across any level, whether you're a new and emerging leader, or a seasoned executive. What I've found is that we rarely take the time to ask, 'What kind of leader do I want to be? What kind of leader am I? What are my personal values, and why are they important?'

It is said that leadership is an inside out job. This is very true. Before you can lead others, you need to be able to lead yourself. You need to ask yourself those questions and find the answers. And once you've found the answers, once you've gained clarity, you need to be able to implement the changes that will allow you to be the kind of leader you do want to be.

Your Clarity Model

To gain clarity you need to understand certain things about yourself, namely:

- Your purpose, and how you can create or build on that purpose in your work and life.
- Your values and ethics.
- Your strengths and weaknesses.
- Your internal and external motivations.
- Your emotional states, both positive and negative, and how those impact on your ability to lead.

Understanding these elements is a process that will not be done in a moment, or even in the course of reading this book. It's a lifelong process. And each time you're presented with a new challenge, a new circumstance or a new role, you'll gain more and more information (or more and more *clarity*) about yourself—about what is important to you and what is not.

But at the end of the day clarity is much more than just a thought exercise. It involves effort, discipline and a firm commitment to your own learning and self-leadership. This includes consciously improving your own leadership skills, day in and day out. You can do this by:

1. Understanding your own strengths and weaknesses and developing the tools to maximise your strengths and optimise your weaknesses.
2. Learning about your own leadership style and how to use that to its best.
3. Developing your passion and focusing your energy to pursue that passion.

4. Creating a methodology for effective goal setting with well-planned execution.

5. Learning to fail and move on.

6. Understanding how you inspire others.

7. Finding your higher purpose.

Improving Your Leadership Skills—Actions that Lead to Clarity

When it comes to leadership there are certain skills that are needed. Many people believe these come down to two things. First, acquiring the relevant technical skills (or learning what you need to know to do your job). And second, hard work. They believe that these efforts will ensure they advance in their career and, importantly, achieve the outcome of becoming a leader.

Unfortunately, just putting in the hard yards is not enough. When it comes to becoming a leader, even the best work ethic or highest technical abilities won't get you all the way. You also need vital soft skills.

These 'soft skills' can worry people. It's often easier to rest in the belief that your work ethic will see you through to the result that you want (leadership). Or to retreat into the idea that you're never going to make your goal because you're not a 'natural leader'. But the good news is that *anyone* can develop these essential soft skills. And in doing so, you gain clarity about yourself, and your own leadership capabilities.

So, how do you develop those leadership skills?

Understand Your Strengths and Weaknesses

There has never been, nor will there ever be, a leader born with everything needed to become a success. Leadership takes time. It takes effort. It takes passion, empathy and care. And to even begin, you need to know exactly what you're working with. You need to understand your strengths and weaknesses.

When you understand your own strengths—whether they are abilities you were born with, or those you've developed over your lifetime—you're able to leverage them for your benefit, to help you become the best leader that you can be and, better yet, the kind of leader that you want to be.

On the other hand, understanding your weaknesses gives you opportunities where you can improve. In fact, addressing your shortcomings lets you experience exponential growth, far more than you would by simply focusing on the things that you're already good at. And even when you see that you might not be able to improve your shortcomings to a place where they can become a strength, you are able to find those people in your team that do have that strength and leverage off of their abilities for the benefit of the entire team.

Learn Your Leadership Style

There's no one right way to lead (there are certainly some wrong ways, however!). It's your prerogative to choose the leadership style that best suits you and your goals for yourself and your team. In general, there are considered to be seven main leadership styles. These are:

1. Autocratic or Authoritative
2. Bureaucratic
3. Democratic of Participative
4. Coaching
5. Transformational or Visionary
6. Servant
7. Laissez-Faire

To learn your leadership style, you can start by taking a test. There are many out there that can help you narrow down where you fall on the spectrum of leadership styles, including one we really like from Atlassian[1].

Once you have a starting point for your own particular leadership style, then you can begin to implement the actions that align with your leadership style. If you are an authoritative leader, perhaps you struggle to listen to input from your team. In this case, you might start practicing ways to engage with and encourage open communication. If you identify as a laissez-faire leader, perhaps you struggle with confidence to actively manage your team. In this case you can begin to find ways to build up your self-confidence and strengthen your management skills. Over time, you'll begin to bring your leadership style into greater alignment with the kind of leader that you want to be, rather than the kind of leader you are right now.

Develop Your Passion

People want to follow leaders who care about their work and about the organisation. They want to follow leaders that are passionate about what they do and about the goals they are seeking. But passion doesn't come easily. It requires effort, exertion and a firm commitment to push on even when things get difficult.

Without passion, the energy will simply drain away from a project and from a goal until pretty soon you find yourself just treading water. You'll cease moving forward, stop innovating and you and your team will stagnate.

---

1   Dupont, Sarah Goff. (2021). 'Discover your natural leadership style with this quiz'. Atlassian. Accessed at https://www.atlassian.com/blog/quiz/find-your-leadership-style-examples.

On the other hand, when you, as a leader, display genuine enthusiasm for your project and goals, that will rub off on your team and the other people around you. It encourages people to put in more focus and more energy to achieve the desired end result because that passion drives them towards the common goal.

Your team will respond positively to your passion. Showing passion for not just the work, but also for everything you do, such as learning new skills and developing new abilities, is an important part of developing your leadership. In fact, while you might be tempted to hide your efforts to develop more or better leadership skills, this is a mistake. Showing your team that you're working hard to improve will inspire them to improve their own leadership and self-leadership as well. And that will be a benefit for the entire organisation.

Set Concrete Goals and Execute Them

The grandest vision will never get off the ground if you don't plot a path to get there. One of the most essential parts of gaining clarity around leadership is clarifying your goals. This means setting concrete goals, not just amorphous plans. And that means goals that are methodical, resourced and committed to.

The first step is to formulate your overall plan. Where are you trying to go and why? Once you have that in place, you need to set methodical, achievable benchmarks. This gives you the beginnings of your roadmap and helps everyone on your team know the path you are following to achieve your goals.

> The grandest vision will never get off the ground if you don't plot a path to get there.

It will guide you along each step. And once you've achieved one step, you'll know just where to head too next.

Achieving these steps along the path to your overall goal gives you and your team small hits of success that will motivate and encourage them and help them feel a sense of purpose and pride.

Fail and Move On

No one is perfect (despite social media's attempts to make us believe otherwise). And no leader is perfect either. Think of the leader you most admire in the world. They're not perfect either. Even the most powerful, effective and inspiring leaders fail. The difference between an effective leader's failure and an ineffective leader's failure is simply in how they handle the failure afterwards.

When an effective leader sees they've made a mistake they never try to cover it up or hide it. They admit it openly and take immediate action to fix it. When necessary, they discuss it with their team so that everyone can learn from the mistake. An effective leader doesn't treat a mistake as something to be ashamed of. They treat it as an opportunity to learn and to better both themselves and others. They ask and then answer the question, 'How can I avoid making this mistake again?'

Once the mistake or the failure has been dealt with an effective leader simply moves on. They don't dwell on the problem or congratulate themselves on fixing it. They simply look towards the next step and move towards that. While there is a benefit to openly discussing your mistakes with your team, there's no additional benefit from beating it to death. Admit it, talk about it, rectify it and then move on.

Inspire Others

You are one of the most important sources of inspiration for the people that you lead. What you say and how you act impacts on the way they do their jobs every day. If you're constantly focusing on the negatives or on seeing the worst-case-scenarios at every turn, people won't be inspired to leap into their work, bringing fresh ideas and innovation. Instead, they'll only feel afraid to make a mistake, worried that their idea might be the one that will bring everything crashing down. When an employee doesn't feel that you believe in them, they're morale crashes and they stop performing well. And once they begin to perform poorly, their morale crashes even further, cementing the negative cycle.

On the other hand, when you are positive, encouraging and supportive, when you foster new ideas and innovations from your team, even if they don't ultimately pan out, then you're inspiring them to work harder and achieve more. Developing this positive leadership mindset is the secret to inspiring your employees and teams. And having inspired teams is the secret to consistent growth in your business.

Find Your Higher Purpose

When developing leadership skills, it's essential that you know why you're putting time and effort into your chosen goal. Ask yourself, what is driving you? What is your higher purpose?

You might start by thinking about some of the basics. A larger paycheck. A better life for your family. A prestigious new role. Yes, those are important motivators for almost everyone. But they certainly aren't your higher purpose.

Take a step back and consider why you want to be a leader. Do you see a place where you can add value? Where you might have the skills and the ability to bring changes into your industry or into the world at large?

Do you feel passionate about something that aligns with your work? Perhaps you want to help other women in your industry succeed. Perhaps you want to work to bring a better life balance to your particular sector. Whatever your higher purpose is, this is the thing that helps you to be confident and clear in why you are doing what you do. It empowers you. And when you convey this to your team and to the organisation, it empowers them as well, both to help you achieve your higher purpose, and to seek out their own.

Flexing your Clarity Muscle

A blueprint is a design or guide that can be followed. If you want to build a great house, you will first need to create a blueprint and follow that design carefully. In the same way, in order to become a great leader, you should draw up a leadership blueprint and follow that design just as carefully.

Just going through the process of creating your own leadership blueprint will make you a better leader because you gain a better understanding and insight of who you are and your strengths and weaknesses. You also begin to see who you want to be, how best to get there and how to support your team every step of the way.

A leadership blueprint is your own individual leadership mission and vision. It helps you to conceptualise what you stand for, what you stand against and what's important to you on your own personal level. Once you have that, you now have your north star to guide you along your own leadership journey.

Your leadership blueprint needs to take into account those that you lead. After all, as a leader, you have a huge responsibility for the people that you lead. There is a waterfall effect of how we show up, and the way we show up as leaders can really impact our team even outside the workplace.

Creating your leadership blueprint

Leadership is a beautiful journey but it's not without its challenges. There's so much more to it than simply having a title and people in your team. Just as life doesn't come with an instruction manual, neither does leadership. So, what's the next best thing? Having a blueprint for your leadership journey.

Here are a few helpful tips to get started.

- Tip 1: Know your leadership style

  Knowing what type of leader, you are is essential for your leadership blueprint. When you better understand yourself, your strengths and your weaknesses, you can better assess the leadership style you should adapt to support and benefit your team.

- Tip 2: Get insights from others

  Speaking to other people and having a courageous conversation™ with them will give you insights about what type of leader you are allowing you to build your leadership blueprint.

- Tip 3: Start journaling

  Journaling is a great tool to get clarity—whether that's in business, your personal life or your relationships. When it comes to refining your own courageous leadership, here are a few self-coaching questions that you can reflect and journal on or choose some others that work best for you. Regardless, give yourself a bit of time and thinking space to reflect on what worked, what didn't and what you want for the future and then implement those into your own leadership blueprint.

Self-Coaching Questions:

What is your mission as a leader?

What is important to you as a leader?

What do you value about others who inspire you?

How do you want to act as a leader?

What do you want to be proud of as a leader?

What are you going to commit to?

What does leadership actually mean to you?

What traits do you value?

What do you expect from your team members?

What do you expect from yourself?

What will you commit to as a leader?

The value of a leadership blueprint

Every one of us has a set of core values, which are key principles and beliefs that we consider important. They influence our decision-making, our actions and behaviours and our personal pleasures. Being conscious of your core principles will also support you in making difficult decisions. Values are normally quite consistent throughout your life, but they might shift over time, particularly in terms of their importance.

We all know there are things we excel at and those we struggle with. This can be viewed from two perspectives:

Perspective 1—Concentrate on your flaws and work to overcome them.

Perspective 2—Focus on your own talents and select partners to match your weaknesses.

Whatever tact you take, you should recognise and accept that you cannot be excellent at everything. Every day is a learning situation for you as you progress further along your chosen path.

Creating a leadership blueprint helps you reflect on what you've done in the past, including both successes and failures and both flaws and talents, and reflect on what you can do and want to do in the future. It enables you to make changes and decisions that can take you a long way towards knowing and achieving those things that are key to being a successful leader.

To download a full Made For More Leadership Blueprint, go to www.madeformore.com.au/resources

Chapter 2

Capability

Made For More: Understanding your ability, what you are capable of and great at and the areas you need to improve in (or backfill) is vital for courageous leadership.

'Excellence is an art won by training and habituation. We do not act rightly because we have virtue or excellence, but we rather have those because we have acted rightly. We are what we repeatedly do. Excellence, then, is not an act but a habit.'

—Aristotle

In leadership, we often hear the words, 'leadership capability', 'capability framework' and 'building capability'. But we aren't often given a framework for building out these capabilities. This leaves us, as leaders, to scrounge for answers ourselves.

But a strong capability framework can be a fantastic tool for career progression. It not only gives you a path to follow, but it creates that path by leveraging the work that incredible people have undertaken before you, implementing things that have worked, and disregarding those that haven't. The right framework will underpin your leadership training, coaching and development and help you to build your leadership capabilities from techniques, systems and processes that have been proven to work to support you. You can think of it as a checklist of sorts, but one that aligns specifically with your specific industry or niche.

Example 1: Public Sector Leadership Capability Framework

For example – a framework in the public sector may consist of 5 overarching capabilities:

- Shaping strategic thinking
- Achieving results
- Cultivating productive working relationships
- Exemplifying personal drive and integrity
- Communicating with influence

Example 2: Start-Up Tech Company Leadership Capability Framework

On the other hand, a framework in a start-up tech company might consist of:

- Thinking strategically
- Engaging people to build positive relationships
- Striving for performance excellence
- Showing courage, resilience, and adaptability
- Leveraging emerging technologies
- Shaping the future

Why Does It Matter

Having the framework to increase your own capabilities as a leader is important. When you find the framework that aligns with your industry, you'll find that you are developing capabilities that represent strategic knowledge and vital attributes and experiences that you need to foster high levels of performance that are in line with your own personal drivers and the organisation's strategic direction. But while this is all well and good, what does it actually mean for the Courageous Leader™?

When working on self-leadership and self-awareness, capability really comes down to knowing what you're good at, what you're great at and what areas you need to improve. We call this—good, great, get better.

Good, Great, Get Better

Good

When your skills are good, that's OK. But you need to continually polish them up to elevate your knowledge and skills, so that you can amplify and capitalise on what you're already good at. As they say, *good is the enemy of great*. And resting on your 'close enough' or 'good enough' laurels won't get you very far in the leadership game.

Brendon Burchard, a three-time New York Times bestselling author, world-renowned high-performance coach and one of the world's most watched personal development trainers, asks his leaders this important question: 'Do you want to be good? Or do you want to be great?'

When you're going for just 'good', you might get there. Or you might get nearly there, leaving you with skills that won't get you where you want to go. After all, nobody will commend you on being just good enough. Nobody reports on 'good'. And courageous leaders certainly don't want 'just good'. They want to be great.

Being great—or taking your skills from just good to great—means commitment. It means telling yourself that you'll do the work you need to do and committing the time, energy, and resources necessary to get you there. It means being firmly focused on *where you are right now*. Not looking to see what else is going on around you. But focused on your role, your skills, your industry and your path to leveraging good to great.

Of course, the most important issue then becomes identifying what you need to *actually* do at a granular, day-in-day-out level–to take yourself from great to good. And that right there is the million-dollar issue.

When I work with leaders who are hovering at 'just good', I start by asking them:

1. Are you happy being good?
2. Or do you want to be great?
3. What do you want to be great at?
4. What daily practice do you need to start to become great at it?
5. What are you already great at that perhaps you've forgotten?
6. What do you find easy and/or enjoyable?

Identifying where you want to be great, what you want to be great at and where you want this to take you is the first step. Then you're in a position to leverage what you're 'just good at' into what you can be absolutely great at.

Great

Most leaders will already be great at some things. But sometimes the skills and capabilities that we're already great at are the hardest to recognise in ourselves.

These areas are sometimes referred to as our genius zones. And you may not even realise what your genius zones are because they come so easily to you. This bias is often referred to as 'unconscious competence' which we'll discuss more in Chapter 10, and even if you aren't able to see these areas of genius for yourself, others will recognise you for these skills and capabilities, which gives you excellent insight into them yourself. In other words, if someone compliments you on your ability to do something well, listen, and take it onboard. They may have just identified something that you're absolutely great at.

Identifying what you're great at, or your genius zones, is important because it helps you identify the gaps in your capabilities. It will highlight where you need to backfill your skills in order to become excellent in every area that you need.

This can be a confronting process. But it's important to remember that everyone—every leader, every team member, every human on this planet—feels a gap between their ordinary lives and the extraordinary lives they want to lead. And that's why it's vital that we adopt the practical steps needed to take us from good to great, and from ordinary to extraordinary.

Get Better (Your Practical Steps to Take You from Good to Great)

Sometimes you may feel you've been doing everything right. You've been working hard, going to the workshops and the seminars, reading the books, taking the classes—in other words, doing all the personal development work that is expected. And while this may have worked for a while, you still may find that you've plateaued. Or you may find that despite all the hard work, you haven't been able to achieve everything that you want for yourself and in your leadership career.

This is where high-performance changes—or going from good to great—needs to happen.

Finding High-Performance Changes

So how do we identify where we can make those high-performance changes—those things that can take us from good to great? Well,

I believe that it comes from identifying our strengths that can be improved, rather than focusing on the things we have no skills in or that are true weaknesses.

Many of us will be familiar with a SWOT analysis—situation, weaknesses, opportunities, threats. SWOT was originally designed to analyse business, or rather business threats, but it has often been applied to the individual as well. It is highly likely that you would have utilised this yourself in one of those many workshops or seminars you've been attending.

The problem with SWOT, and the reason that I don't believe there's much benefit for us as leaders, is that under its framework we usually end up focusing on our weaknesses, rather than on polishing up what we're naturally or already good at. Finding and fixing people's 'weaknesses' is the traditional approach to workplace and leadership development and is likely one that you've experienced first-hand. However, this methodology only ends up giving a poor employee experience which is underpinned by mediocre improvements and a significant drop in engagement[2].

On the other hand, focusing on 'your strengths unlocks your potential and leads you to greater performance'[3]. *Gallup's* research shows that when we focus on our weaknesses, we *might* get an 8% uplift[4]. However, if we focus on improving our strengths, there's a notable 18% increase in performance[5].

---

2   Strengths Development & Coaching. *Gallup.* Accessed at https://www.gallup.com/learning/248405/strengths-development-coaching.aspx.

3   'Live Your Best Life Using Your Strengths'. *Gallup,* Clifton Strengths. Accessed at https://www.gallup.com/cliftonstrengths/en/252137/home.aspx?utm_source=-google&utm_medium=cpc&utm_campaign=australia_cs_ecom&utm_term=gal-lup%20strengths&gclid=CjwKCAiArOqOBhBmEiwAsgeLmQIuobSlapODDQ5rrk-gddEwmVKLjm5b4hhBcAcW4EjOS3GY7tzIt0BoCbfQQAvD_BwE.

4   Ibid.

5   Ibid.

> You don't need to have all of the answers, you just need to know where to find them.

Unless an area of weakness is a fundamental part of your role (and if that's the case, I suspect you probably don't love the work that you do), you can successfully manage weaknesses by simply recruiting someone who loves and has a strength in the area that you don't. By taking this approach you'll be strengthening your own areas of expertise, as well as your new teammates, and providing an avenue for you both to gain more confidence and become more productive and self-aware.

At the end of the day, you don't need to have all of the answers, you just need to know where to find them.

Finding Your Own Strengths

Answer the following questions to learn about your own leadership strengths:

1.   When there is a conflict in my team I:

    a.   Remind them of our strategic goals
    b.   Bring them together to talk it out
    c.   Let them work it out themselves

2.   I ensure my team meet their goals by:

    a.   Delegating often with clear, unmistakable instructions
    b.   Encouraging everyone's participation
    c.   Leading by example and working towards the individual, team, and organisational goals

3. When I have a team member who is highly skilled, motivated, and productive, I:

    a. Ensure they are adhering to the same strategies and processes as the other members of the team

    b. Ask them to have creative collaboration meetings with me

    c. Leave them alone to do their work

4. If I notice that a team member is unmotivated, I:

    a. Closely manage their tasks to make sure they're doing everything by the book

    b. Make the extra effort to bring them into team discussions and voice their opinions and ideas

    c. Let them have some space

5. When I have a new team member I:

    a. Manage them directly until they understand our processes, requirements, and expectations

    b. Invite them to collaborate with the team through meetings and projects

    c. Let them find their own best way of working with the team

6. If I need to create a new marketing strategy, I:

    a. Create the strategy myself and then advise the team

    b. Take the challenge directly to the team for suggestions and ideas

    c. Hand the project over to the team and ask them to come back with a plan

7. If we have a project with a tight deadline, I:

    a. Issue instructions and deadlines to each member to ensure we meet the project's deadline

     b.   Advise what the project is as well as the deadline and leave them to it

     c.   Ask them for their advice on the best way to meet the difficult deadline

8. I trust my team members:

     a.   Not at all

     b.   A fair amount

     c.   Very much

9. Poor performance should be:

     a.   Punished to ensure that it doesn't happen again

     b.   Talked through with learnings explored

     c.   Pointed out to the team member who is then given space to work it out themselves

10. When it comes to making decisions, I:

     a.   Make a decision and then advise the team what that decision is

     b.   Ask for input from the team and then make a decision

     c.   Let my team make the decisions

If you answered mostly 'a's then you have a mostly authoritarian leadership style. The benefit of this style is that you likely have a good idea of the big picture and an excellent strategic approach. You're also likely to make good decisions under pressure. Where you might be lacking is in creative ideas gathering and also trusting others.

If you answered mostly 'b's then you have a participative leadership style. The benefit of this style is that you demonstrate that you value your team by including them often, and you are able to gather good creative input and fresh ideas. The difficulty here is learning how to manage differing opinions once you've invited participation. Also, the decision-making could become very slow, which is another factor you'll need to learn to manage.

If you answered mostly 'c's then you're a laissez-faire leader, which means that you let people do as they like. One of this style's greatest benefits is how well you empower your team to make decisions with little or no guidance. But this is also one of the biggest downsides, and you'll need to ensure you have the skills to support your team as they take on these responsibilities.

These leadership styles don't necessarily point out what skills you have—but they *tend to* indicate where you have strengths and where you don't. It's a great place to start when working out how to embrace your own strengths to grow your own leadership capabilities.

The Capabilities of the Courageous Leader™

Often referred to as the 'soft skills' in leadership, there are some capabilities (regardless of your leadership style, or individual strengths and weaknesses) that will put you on the right path to becoming a Courageous Leader™

Vulnerability

"Vulnerability is the birthplace of innovation, creativity and change."

—Brené Brown

Vulnerability has received quite a bit of airtime recently, although I believe it's for all the wrong reasons. Vulnerability is not about airing all your dirty laundry. Instead, it should be about sharing your experiences, your story, and your challenges with the people you lead. In other words, to show the 'real' side of you.

Too often those in a leadership position are perceived as 'unreachable'. And this puts a barrier between you and your team or even your colleagues because they 'don't want to say something silly in front of the boss'. While you and I know that you're a very real person, does your team know?

Years ago, when I was still working at the credit union, we had a coin sorting machine. People would come in and dump their coins into the machine which would then sort them out into various denominations and put them into a safe within the bank. The safe was very heavy and we had to wheel it into the back safe every night, and then wheel it back out the next morning.

One morning after a very stressful couple of weeks it was time to move the coin safe to its daytime spot but for some reason it just wouldn't go in. This safe weighed a tonne, often full of people's spare change, plus the weight of the physical safe and it was on tiny castor wheels. I was shoving it and shoving it and trying to keep my cool and shoving it a bit more. But I just could not get the wheels to line up. And as I was shoving and shoving it, I was getting more and more frustrated inside.

I was trying to keep it professional (after all I was wearing the leadership hat) but I finally lost my cool and gave it a bit of a kick. Of course, kicking a solid safe isn't really a great idea, and as you can imagine it had no effect at all. So, I gave it one last shove, burst into tears and walked out of the office. We hadn't even opened yet.

Once I was out of the office, I collected myself and gave myself a stern talking to. And then I put my leadership mask back on and walked back in. Not long after that I was approached by one of the women that I worked with. She was one of those that I'd had a really hard time connecting with until now, and as she came up to me, I metaphorically put up my defences–I just knew that I was really going to be in for it. But I was wrong.

This woman wasn't there to give me a talking to or to poke at my weaknesses. Instead, what she said was how nice it was to see me get upset. She said, 'When you lost your cool it actually showed me that you were a real person.' Turns out that up until then she'd thought that I was emotionally detached from everything. And she hadn't realised just how stressed out I was. And when I had a little bit of a meltdown it showed her that I could be (and was) vulnerable, too.

That moment had a huge impact in turning around my relationship with this particular staff member and greatly benefited how we worked together. So, while it wasn't necessarily my finest moment, and I certainly wouldn't encourage you to kick a safe, by showing that softer side of myself I was able to have a profound leadership experience that taught me how important vulnerability truly is.

Many years later, vulnerability came into the forefront with the work of

Brené Brown. But leaders, through their own experiences, would have understood this intuitively long before.

Authenticity

Authenticity really refers to your leadership image. In other words, what are you known for? What level is yourself awareness? What are your values (and are you living them every day)? Do you do what you say you're going to do? And are you able to lead without wearing your armour (the way we shield ourselves from shame, vulnerability or emotional exposure in the world)?

When it comes down to authentic leadership, being authentic is about leading in your own way. If you try to lead like someone else, then you will simply fail. Your team won't follow you if they sense that your leadership behaviours are forced, manipulated or simply not 'real'. On the other hand, showing up authentically drives the belief that you're sincere, honest and truthful, and it's an attribute that defines all great leaders.

The challenge here is finding the balance between expressing your personality (authentically) and managing your team. If, for example, one of your authentic strengths is your ability to be direct, you will need to find a way to continue to embrace your forthrightness while navigating the complexity of a political environment. It's not easy, but unless you can do so, you'll leave your team confused and languishing in distrust.

Authentic leadership is revealed in the alignment of what you think, what you say, and what you do.'—Michael Holland, Founder and President, Bishop House

Empathy

Empathy is another quality that seems to be getting more and more airtime. In fact, I ran a leadership executive summit recently and one of our core topics was managing empathy and productivity.

For years, productivity and output have been the measure of successful leadership. However, with the disruption of COVID, and our new ways of working, empathy has supplanted output as a fundamental leadership skill that leaders need to lean into. That's not to say that output and outcomes are no longer important–they are. But what has changed is that output is no longer *at the expense* of empathy and compassion.

Years ago, I was working with a dentist who said, 'Ally, I don't really *do* empathy'. As you can imagine, being a dentist, he came into contact all day long with people who were highly anxious, in pain or otherwise upset and emotional. And while he didn't see empathy as an important part of his work, his patients certainly did. By not having this soft skill he lessened his desirability as a dentist, which meant an impact on his bottom line (something he could certainly understand). In his case, empathy was definitely a muscle that needed flexing.

Like this dentist, many leaders struggle with empathy. But in this case, you actually *can* fake it until you make it. Begin by making the right noises, thinking about their perspective and considering how you might like to be treated if you were in their shoes. Over time you'll start to get a better sense of what your team might be feeling, and this will naturally develop and strengthen your empathy muscle.

Tenacity (Continual development)

I'm lucky enough to work with some exceptional people and leaders. And the one thing they all have in common is that they haven't stopped learning, growing, developing or asking for help. This is tenacity, and it's a vital capability of courageous leaders.

Tenacity means continually striving for what's next. It means seeking out a greater level of connection and working towards creating a larger impact. It means committing to this leadership gig, and giving it all you've got with determination, resilience, grit and persistence.

Tenacity is a vital capability of leaders. In fact, it's described by Nancy Eberhardt, executive coach and CEO of Pathwise Partners in *Forbes*, as the 'single greatest factor for success' which can 'take a team from doing all right to thriving'. This is the ability to persevere despite challenges, and to learn from mistakes so you can try again. So, it doesn't mean not failing. Instead, it means failing and trying again until you finally do succeed.

Today's world is often about quick fixes and immediate ROIs. So, when things get challenging, or messy, or we're met with failure, too often people walk away. Great, courageous leaders embrace those challenges, communicating with authenticity and candour and finding solutions with long-term focus and methodologies. And that's tenacity.

Kindness

I want to talk in this section about kindness is king, kindness vs niceness.

At some stage you have probably been told to be nice. What's really important not just as a leader but as a life skill is kindness. You might be wondering what the difference is, and I think the difference is really in the actions rather than the words. Niceness generally involves doing something that is pleasing or agreeable, it's self fulfilling. Kindness on the other hand is going something that is helpful to others or comes from a place of benevolence. Being nice is superficial, being kind isn't always being nice. Kindness gives permission for real success, and real failure. Kindness is about understanding rather than appeasing.

The 3 Gs – Grunt, Grit & Grace™

I was recently asked by someone what connects all those years on the stage to what I do now working with leaders, teams and organisations. I admit, the answer stumped me for a little while. But then I realised that it all comes back to the 3 Gs:

- Grunt
- Grit
- Grace

Grunt

You can think of grunt as the physical and mental work of dancing. It's the learning, the study and the heavy lifting. For dance this meant learning the positions and the steps. Understanding the moves. Becoming aware of how the body works and can be developed to accomplish amazing things.

In leadership, grunt is much the same. It's the heavy lifting of responsibility. It's learning about yourself, your team, your strategies and goals. It's understanding where strengths and weaknesses are, and how to motivate your element of the organisation (yourself and your team) to be better, stronger and more fluid. It's the foundational work that gives you little to no reward—at least not at first. But gives you the strength to begin the real practice of leadership.

This is the grunt work of leadership, the heavy lifting, the heavy duty thinking, the heavy responsibility.

Grit

Grit, on the other hand, is the practice of leadership. It's no surprise that leadership is hard work. It's putting in the hours. It's learning on the job. It's failing (fast) and moving on. It's being 100% accountable. And it's practice, every single day.

Grit is a little bit like holding on (for dear life). If I think back to my years in the studio and on the stage, grit was the process of falling over and getting up again. Grit was doing the same step or routine over and over again until it was right and ingrained in our body.

We used to have a saying– *'learn 5th to forget it'*. 5th position is one way of positioning the feet that any dancer would be able to show you no matter how long they've been off the stage. We practiced it so frequently because we needed to be able to do it without thinking about it. We needed to be able to 'forget it' or stop thinking about it, so that it became a part of who we were, like breathing. And that took grit.

Grace

Finally, grace. Grace is the bit that people see. One of the most famous ballets is Swan Lake. Swans are often described as graceful and the dancers in Swan Lake are required to show that same gracefulness in every one of their moves, whether it's the strongest lift or jump, or the smallest wave of their fingers. But what the audience doesn't see is what's gone on behind the scenes, under the surface.

They don't see the sheer muscle strength required to make a jump and land it perfectly. They don't understand the determination it takes to hold one position and then fall into the next as if it took nothing more than a slight wind to blow the dancer over. Every movement takes hundreds of precise muscle movements and an incredible focus. But because it looks so graceful, sometimes it even looks easy.

Grace in leadership is the same way. It looks easy from the outside, but it's the end result of being supported by incredible foundational work, immense capabilities and skills obtained through years of practice, sweat and even tears. But to the audience (your team) it simply looks like being able to take the high road. Like being able to let the water flow down your back and carry on despite challenges, setbacks or failures. Of course, as the leader you know the truth. But the true benefit of grace is that you feel it's benefit, too, though you know that it's the result of all those other elements that came before.

Flexing Your Capability Muscle

Now that you have the tools to understand the skills you've already mastered, what you're capable of and great at and the areas that might be weaknesses, you're in a fantastic position to flex your capability muscles. You're also in a great position to backfill those areas that you may need some help with.

This is a lifelong journey, and your work on your own courageous leadership will never be done. But that doesn't mean you can't make great strides each and every day. Using grunt (hard work), grit (persistence) and grace (hard-earned ease) will help you become the leader you want to be, and the leader your team and organisation deserve.

Chapter 3

Confidence

Made For More Definition: The Ability to show passion for their beliefs and values, while demonstrating consistent and predictable behaviour.

> "A flower does not think of competing with the flower next to it, it just blooms."

—Zen Shin

Confidence and Leadership

One of the biggest struggles leaders face is imposter syndrome. Imposter syndrome, or the feeling that you just aren't good enough (and everyone is going to find out!), is really just a lack of confidence in disguise.

The thing about imposter syndrome is that its very nature contributes to the feeling that you're the only one to experience it (that you're the one who's on the out, who's not good enough, who's the fraud). But actually, it's incredibly common. Research shows that 70% of people experience imposter syndrome[6], both men and women and across all walks of life and industries. In fact, it can affect anyone who isn't able to 'internalise and own their own successes'[7]. And the real kicker is that they don't often recognise it.

So, how do you recognise it for what it is? Well, when you suffer from imposter syndrome whenever you have success, you question whether

---

6   Sakulku, Jaruwan. 'The Imposter Phenomenon'. *International Journal of Behavioural Science*. 6(1), 75–97. Accessed at https://doi.org/10.14456/ijbs.2011.6
7   Abrams, Abigail. 'Yes, Impostor Syndrome Is Real. Here's How to Deal With It'. *Time*. 20 June 2018. Accessed at https://time.com/5312483/how-to-deal-with-impostor-syndrome/.

you can do it again. You wonder if it was just a fluke. And you often find yourself waiting for that tap on the shoulder. For someone to call you out for not being who you say you are. Or for being 'accidentally successful'.

When you suffer from imposter syndrome, whenever you've been asked to 'come for a quick chat', your immediate response is to think, 'Oh no. What have I done?', rather than, 'Great! I was hoping we could touch base.

If you have felt these feelings, that's imposter syndrome.

At its most basic level, imposter syndrome comes down to a misalignment of your confidence, with your success or abilities. Often when I'm working with leaders, they're looking to increase their confidence, and this is also the best way to combat imposter syndrome. As a first step, increasing confidence requires leaders to take action.

Fake It Til You Make It

There's the saying of fake it til you make it. And when it comes to building confidence, this is absolutely true.

Neurologically our brains can't tell the difference between what we *think* is real, and what we *know* to be real. Another way of thinking about it is that our life experience, and our expectations (and even desires/wants), influence the stories that our minds tell us. A great example is how political partisans see the facts of current events differently depending on their political viewpoints. The reality of the world is altered in their perspective[8]. In the same way, your own internal reality is altered based on what your life experiences and beliefs tell you.

---

8   Resnick, Brian. '"Reality" is constructed by your brain. Here's what that means, and why it matters.' 22 June 2020. Vox. Accessed at https://www.vox.com/science-and-health/20978285/optical-illusion-science-humility-reality-polarization.

This gives us a fantastic opportunity to build our own level of confidence, just by faking confidence. Amy Cuddy in her TEDx Talk talks about power poses and their ability to build up confidence. While this can sound a little silly, the science behind power posing is profound. Cuddy's research (which has been further supported by a systematic review and meta-analysis conducted by Emma Elkjær with colleagues from Aarhus, Witten/Herdecke and Columbia Universities in 2020[9]) shows that when people assume an open or expansive stance, when they make themselves appear taller and wider, then they feel more powerful. And when they *feel* more powerful, they believe they *are* more powerful.

It's important to remember that confidence is not optimism. While optimism is the belief that everything is going to be okay., confidence is believing that *you* will be OK, even if things aren't. For our purposes that definition is expanded to believing that you have the leadership skills necessary to support yourself and your team whether or not things are okay.

As a leader, faking that confidence—not just to your team, but to yourself as well—is a vital first step.

Building a Leadership Vision

Faking it, even understanding that this is going to help change your perspective, is only going to take you so far. You also need to begin taking action that can build your confidence from an objective point of view. In order to build confidence as a leader, you need to get clear on your leadership vision, and then take steps to act on their vision. Each action will build micro beliefs in your leadership abilities and in your competency to tackle what comes next.

---

9   Elkjær, E., Mikkelsen, M.B., Michalak, J. et al. 'Expansive and contractive postures and movement: A systematic review and meta-analysis of the effect of motor displays on affective and behavioural responses.' 2020. Perspectives on Psychological Science. doi:10.1177/1745691620919358

What is Leadership Vision

Your leadership vision will be specific to you, your organisation, your team and your industry. But no matter what those specifics are, in general it is the capacity to see your current situation clearly, understand what inspiring future you're aiming to achieve and have a strategy to achieve it.

4 Ways to Build Your Leadership Vision

Building your leadership vision can happen in any number or ways, but here are four you might consider:

1. **Leverage internal vision.** Take a look around your team and organisation for those people that have a high degree of vision and the ability to think strategically.
2. **Stop working on the day-to-day execution.** Pull yourself out of the day-to-day work of planning and executing, in order to give yourself space to focus on the strategic outlook.
3. **Find inspiration.** Look to people who are visionary leaders and follow their examples. Visionary leaders approach problems and solutions differently and when you're building your leadership vision, this strategic, out-of-the-box thinking is vital.
4. **Ask forward-looking questions.** Get your team together and ask them questions. For example, 'What direction are we moving, and why? Does it fit our mission? What are we hoping to achieve in the next 12 months, three years or even 10 years?' The questions and answers will both help to form your own vision and strategy.

Once you've built your leadership vision, you need to be prepared to take the action to implement that vision. Taking action to support your leadership vision will allow you to build and grow your leadership confidence. And you'll be in a position to take more (and better) targeted actions in the future that can lead to even greater success (and more and better confidence).

When we lack confidence, we prefer to stay inactive. As humans it's the equivalent of spending days on the couch, in our PJs, watching Netflix. While this can be great occasionally (mental health matters), if as a leader you're doing metaphorical couch surfing all the time, it simply reaffirms any lack of confidence you might be feeling. And the more you stay inactive, the more confidence you will lose.

Confidence means having enough belief in our own abilities that we're willing to take some steps, some action, even when we're not 100% sure that we're going to be successful. That's when we *fake it til we make it*.

Hurdles to Confidence

Once you spend time wrestling with your own self-doubt or imposter syndrome, you will come to realise that many of the hurdles to confidence you face actually come from inside your own head. If you can take those apart, then any external factors are much easier to face.

So, what are those hurdles to confidence?

Don't want to be seen as bossy, arrogant or aggressive

Often leaders worry about being too confident (or acting too confident) feeling that it may portray them as bossy, arrogant or aggressive. But it is vital to understand that confidence, or self-confidence, is quite different to perceived aggression. And research shows that they are separated by one thing—empathy.

While there is a fine line between arrogance and confidence, an arrogant person feels they must assert themselves to feel superior, while a confident person knows their worth and doesn't feel a need to prove it. An arrogant person asserts their power regardless of the impact it has on those around them, while a confident person doesn't feel a need to defend their position and takes the time to feel the needs of others. And an arrogant person allows their ego to determine their actions, while a confident person has the internal flexibility that allows in others and their ideas.

For leaders, it's important to be confident but never arrogant. Research shows that working for arrogant leaders has multiple negative effects on team member performance, self-esteem and morale[10]. It results in lower self-confidence (in you as the leader, and in your team) and can lead to less ethical behaviour[11]. And it leads to lower retention.

Arrogant leaders are just not good for business, and when left unchecked, can be a destructive force in any organisation.

Leaders can (and should) show their softer side (Compassion, see Chapter 7) and still be confident. You can stand by your opinions, defend your point of view and stay true to your morals through confidence and empathy—you don't need arrogance or ego.

---

10   Riggio, Ronald E. 'Why Arrogance Could Be Hurting Your Organization'. Psychology Today. 17 June 2019. Accessed at https://www.psychologytoday. com/us/blog/cutting-edge-leadership/201906/why-arrogance-could-be-hurting-your-organization?eml.

11   McGuffin, Ken. 'Sagging confidence can lead to more self-interested behaviour -- or less, Rotman study finds.' University of Toronto. 22 March 2018. Accessed at https://www.rotman.utoronto.ca/Connect/MediaCentre/NewsReleases/20180322.

Struggling under imposter syndrome

We've spoken about imposter syndrome, but it remains one of the biggest hurdles to leadership confidence. And that's because it's an ongoing struggle. Even when you think you understand imposter syndrome, and have battled it into submission, it may suddenly burst back in when you least expect it. (When you're meeting new people at an event, for example. Or explaining a new strategy you would like to implement.) And when it does, it makes you feel powerless, and takes you right back to the beginning of your confidence journey.

Struggling under the imposter syndrome means constantly fighting to keep it in its place, to remind yourself of your successes and truly see them for what they are.

Dealing with the itty bitty committee

Everyone has negative, self-sabotaging, critical voices they carry around in their heads. They're called the itty bitty committee. These are your inner voices, or inner thoughts, that like to chime in whenever you're about to undertake anything that challenges you, is new or big in your life or work. They are critical, reminding you of all the times (real or perceived) that you've failed or messed up in the past, and all the ways (real or perceived) that you can fail or mess up in the future.

The itty bitty committee is, unfortunately, pretty powerful. There is anecdotal talk that 80% of all our thoughts are negative. While I haven't been able to corroborate that number with scholarly research[12], there's a reason it's such a widely held belief. That's because it rings true.

---

12   This is regularly cited as being reported by the National Science Foundation. However, the NSF is a funding body and doesn't complete research themselves, and despite copious research, if the study does exist, it is not available to be found.

What is absolutely scientifically proven is that our minds have the tendency to focus on the negative, and to play the same negative thoughts on repeat, over and over[13]. Your itty bitty committee is a big part of that negative bandwidth. And if you don't do something about it, they can become more and more powerful over time.

In combating their impact, it helps to pay *more* attention to those voices (that committee) than before. Notice them, note what they're saying. This sounds contradictory, but in paying attention and recognising them for what they are, you are able to disempower them to a much bigger extent. And once you do that, you're able to assert your own, independent voice and put them where they belong.

Systemic low confidence

It makes sense that having systemic low confidence will inhibit you from developing confidence in your leadership. You might also think of this as low-self-esteem. Low self-esteem is different from the imposter syndrome, because, rather than a belief that you aren't as good as you say you are, or that you're a fraud, it's a belief that you lack the general ability to succeed. Imposter syndrome can often flow from low self-esteem, of course, but the main thrust of low confidence or low self-esteem is that it prevents you from aiming high enough to progress.

'Reach for the moon. Even if you miss, you'll land among the stars'.

Years ago, when I first started with the Australian Classical Youth Ballet Company, we rehearsed in a

---

13   Kelly IV, John D. 'Your Best Life: Managing Negative Thoughts—The Choice is Yours.' *Clin Orthop Relat Res.* June 2019. Accessed at https://www.nature.com/articles/s41398-019-0560-0.

transportable ballet studio right in the heart of the city. The space was shared with arts students as well, and in true creative fashion, they had painted a mural on one of the internal studio walls. It read, 'Reach for the moon. Even if you miss, you'll land among the stars'. Each day, as I read this wall having just finished a gruelling eight-hour rehearsal, I became more and more aware of just how true this was for every area of life.

When we aim high, we're bound to hit something amazing. But if we don't, then we certainly will find ourselves falling short of our potential.

When you find yourself with low self-esteem or low confidence, remind yourself of this. Not trying is the surest way to fail. Backing yourself by aiming high is the only way to succeed. Envision what you want, and you'll know what to work for. And you might just get there.

Where does confidence come from?

An experiment by psychologist David Dunning suggests that our genetic makeup determines up to 50% of our confidence. The other 50% is formed by personal experience[14]. So, those born with high-confidence genes will likely maintain high confidence regardless of external inputs while they're growing up, while those who are not born with the genes, will certainly struggle more. However, results will also depend on what experiences you've had in your life and how they've shaped you.

So, while it's true that we're predisposed for high or low confidence, and that our experiences up until this point will also seriously impact on our confidence levels, the good news is that we can gather new experiences now that can help build up our confidence once again. In other words, you can teach yourself to be confident.

---

14   Dunning, David (2005). Self-insight: Roadblocks and Detours on the Path to Knowing Thyself. New York: Psychology Press. Accessed at https://www.taylor-francis.com/books/mono/10.4324/9780203337998/self-insight-david-dunning. pp. 14–15. ISBN 978-1841690742. OCLC 56066405.

Here's how to do just that.

Reign in the itty bitty committee

This first step is by reigning in the itty bitty committee. By consciously stopping those automatic negative thoughts (or ANTs), and replacing them with positive thoughts, you are able to create alternative thought patterns. These alternative thought patterns allow you to avoid slipping into ANTs and help you build your level of confidence.

The best way to do this is by putting good old-fashioned pen to paper.

Ask yourself, 'What is it that I'm telling myself?' Then follow it with how you could reframe or replace that thought with a positive one.

Use the table below to help you clarify your ANTs and reframe or replace them to create a positive thought pattern.

Adverse Event	ANTs	Reframe/Replace
Example: Boss calls you into their office out of the blue	*Example:* I'm going to get fired.	*Example:* My boss often calls me into his office to speak about projects
Example: You made a mistake.	*Example:* I'm probably going to get in trouble. I'm no good at this job.	*Example:* What can I learn from this? What can I do next time to make sure this doesn't happen?
Example: You missed out on a promotion	*Example:* I'm not good enough to be here. I'm going nowhere in life	*Example:* I can ask for feedback on where I can improve next time.

Keep promises to yourself

When you want to build up your own confidence, especially as a courageous leader, it's important that you keep your own promises to yourself. How often have you said, 'Today I'm going to go for a walk at lunch rather than eat at my desk.' Or 'This week I'm going to eat healthy.' Or, 'I'm going to have that date night with my partner.' And how often have you failed to meet that promise?

When we're busy the first person that we tend to let down is ourselves. That's because breaking promises to ourselves is far easier than letting down someone at work, or missing a client deadline, for example. But it's also one way that we can seriously undermine our own confidence in our abilities. Broken promises are the thieves of confidence.

Mel Robbins, author of *The 5 Second Rule: Transform your Life, Work, and Confidence with Everyday Courage*, says, 'Keeping promises to yourself is a key aspect of your identity, and builds your confidence. When you keep promises to yourself, it boosts your confidence where you feel compelled to attempt even bigger and bolder things. You develop your own success formula, what works uniquely for you.'

In order to ensure that you keep your promises to yourself, develop a plan of how you're going to do it. Do you have the time and resources you need? Is it something that you really want? Or is it just a promise to keep that's important to someone else? Have you shared your promise with someone? Committing out loud to a friend can make you feel vulnerable. However, it helps to have someone to support and encourage you and pull you up when your promises start to slip.

Understanding your Locus of Control

Julian Rotter coined the term 'Locus of Control' in the 1950s[15], which simply describes our individual perceptions about the underlying causes of events in our lives. In other words, do you believe that the things that have happened to you, and will happen to you in the future, are controlled by external forces, such as fate or family dynamics or even Religious or Spiritual beliefs? This is an external Locus of Control. Or do you believe that you have the power to control your own destiny? This is an internal Locus of Control?

Generally, people that have a stronger internal Locus of Control, or a feeling that they have greater self-agency and self-determination, fare better in life. They tend to achieve more, have better paying lives and cultivate a personal sense of confidence[16].

Look for the friendly mirrors

In Noah St. John's book, *The Secret Code of Success: 7 Hidden Steps to More Wealth and Happiness,* he talks about the idea that only confident people ever 'get more confidence'. While growing your confidence seems easy in theory, especially when you're already inclined towards confidence, it can be a struggle for others who aren't.

St John advises that if you have low self-confidence or are lacking in confidence, you look for the friendly mirrors. That means find those around you that you can trust, who believe in you and who say wonderful

---

15   Rotter, Julian B. 'Generalized expectancies for internal versus external control of reinforcement.' Psychological monographs. Accessed at https://www.semantic-scholar.org/paper/Generalized-expectancies-for-internal-versus-of-Rotter/161c-b7ac92d7571042bb11ebdaaa1175be8079f8.
16   Neill, James. 'What is Locus of Control?' USMCU. Undated. https://www.usmcu.edu/Portals/218/What%20is%20Locus%20of%20Control%20by%20James%20Neill.pdf.

things about you. Look for those people, gather them around you, and rely on them to give you a boost when you need it.

This is not to say that you should surround yourself with sycophants or yes men. Instead, find those people that generally admire you (they exist) and want to see well. And while this is a great step, you'll also need to learn to look at the evidence on your own winning past performance and fantastic confidence-building experiences in order to be your own friendly mirror.

Don't give up

I'm often reminded of the power of determination (grit!) when I watch my kids trying (and trying) to attempt something new.

With four young children, I've spent a fair amount of time coaxing and waiting for them to crawl, walk, say their first word and write their name (among many other things). What comes to mind in particular is my third baby. He's four years old now, but as a toddler he was very determined to walk. Yet try as he might, for months he just couldn't get it.

He'd pull himself up, and plop back down, only to get back up and try again. Of course, as a four-year-old he's very agile now. But can you imagine if he just gave up as an infant, saying, 'That's it, I'm not going to try walking anymore. I failed. It's no use'.

Of course, none of us are toddlers and as adults our failures feel much bigger. But the central message remains the same. Don't give up. Try again. And then try again.

Flexing Your Confidence Muscle

At the end of the day, confidence is an essential part of leadership. A confident leader thinks positively about the future. They're willing to take risks to achieve goals. They have the vision and courage to see that vision come to life[17]. And if that doesn't convince you, a study out of Melbourne University found that confidence is a 'key determinant of workplace success'[18].

So, overcoming your confidence hurdles, like imposter syndrome or the itty bitty committee is about more than just feeling good. It can actually make you better at your job and more successful in your career. Sounds like a goal worth pursuing.

17   Bacha, Zina. 'Leadership Success: Why Self-Confidence is Vital for Leaders.' Strammer. 20 May 2021. Accessed at https://strammer.com/en/why-self-confi-dence-is-vital-for-leaders/.

18   University of Melbourne. 'Self-confidence the secret to workplace advance-ment.' ScienceDaily. 18 October 2012. Accessed at www.sciencedaily.com/releas-es/2012/10/121018103214.htm.

Chapter 4

Leading To Inspire

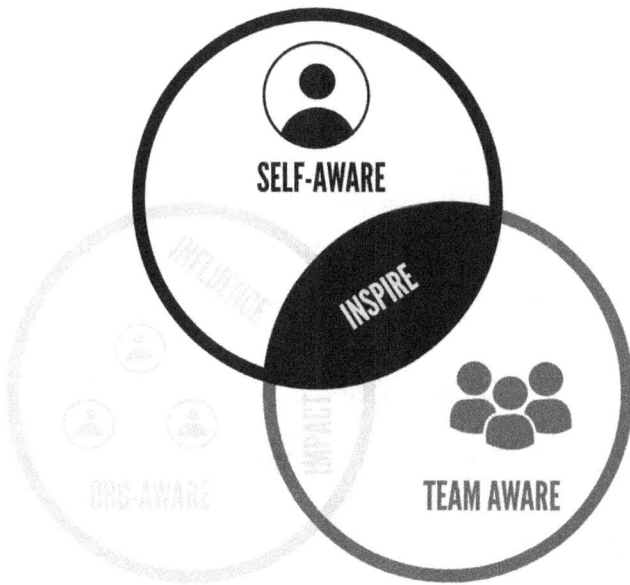

Made For More definition: Leaders need to be able to inspire their teams, have a clear and compelling vision. Don't always align strategically and may feel underappreciated or perhaps don't get the bigger picture.

> "Lead and inspire people. Don't try to manage and manipulate people. Inventories can be managed but people must be led."

> —Ross Parrot

Leaders need to be able to inspire their teams with a clear and compelling vision. But teams don't always align strategically or emotionally engage with the leader's vision. When they don't get the bigger picture, this may lead them to feel underappreciated.

Self-Aware + Team Aware = Inspiring

People, especially leaders, often use the terms 'inspire' and 'motivate' interchangeably. Conceptually they may seem related. However, they are, in fact, worlds apart.

Inspire

'Inspire' translates to "in spirit'. In other words, it's an inspiration which comes from within. It's different from motivation, which *pushes* you towards a course of action. When you are *inspired* by a person, an event or a circumstance, you are *pulled* towards something. This thing stirs your heart, mind or spirit–compelling you to act because of your own internal pull. It's an intrinsic, internal driver.

When we are inspired, we aren't necessarily worried about the end result at all. Instead, our goal is to hold onto that feeling that's filled us for as long as possible. And our internal driver (rather than any external motivation) does the work of moving us towards that goal. That internal feeling of purpose and meaning is all that we need to keep us moving along the path.

In contrast, when we are not inspired, we have to find other methods and other drivers to keep ourselves moving forward towards a specific goal. When we don't have a clear mission or purpose, when we don't understand (or care) why we're doing what we're doing, this external motivation often has to be quite high in order to keep us moving. This is why the most effective leaders are the most inspired leaders. Because their inspiration is a far more compelling reason to keep on doing what we're doing.

Motivate

On the other hand, the root word for 'motivate' is 'motive'. A motive is best understood as an external force that causes someone to take action. If inspiration is an internal force that pulls from within, you can think of motivation push that drives you to meet a specific end goal, even when you would rather be doing something else. In terms of your team, this might be meeting monthly KPIs, or daily sales targets, or some other task or event altogether.

I'm often asked, 'How can I motivate my team more?' The short answer is, you can't. What you can do is create an *environment* of motivation.

Each of your team will have different drivers and motivators. Being able to identify those, and build incentives around their own individual and group motivations will build an environment of motivation. This involves understanding the different kinds of motivation, and how to best use them to help your team to achieve.

There's two main types of motivation to be aware of:

1. **Intrinsic Motivation**—Intrinsic motivation moves you to do something from within. It is doing something without expecting rewards, and it's generally more satisfying and enjoyable.

2. **Extrinsic Motivation**—Extrinsic motivation moves you to do something as a result of a reward, such as acknowledgement, money, promotion or the like. Extrinsic motivation comes from external sources, and it is generally not as satisfying or enjoyable.

Extrinsic Motivation (Outcome of the result)	Intrinsic Motivation (Enjoyment in the task)
Win awards for awards sake	Want to reach their full potential
Work to get paid or for acknowledgment	Work without expecting awards
Have an individual goal	Have a common purpose

While being inspired is the most efficient drivers for a team, internal motivation is preferable to external motivation. That's because extrinsically motivated staff are more likely to do a task because it's necessary (or a required part of their job) rather than because they like it or feel fulfilled by completing it.

On the other hand, intrinsically motivated staff are more likely to do a task because they understand it's purpose and feel good about doing it. They completion of the task itself fulfils something internally within them.

In Daniel Pink's *New York Time*'s best-selling book, *Drive,* he discusses research completed at MIT[19]. This research found that extrinsic motivational techniques are effective for simple, routine tasks. However, when tasks required higher cognitive functions or innovation, extrinsic motivates were no longer effective. Instead, these higher-level tasks required people who were motivated by a sense of autonomy, mastery and meaning because they tended to do better at complex problem-solving.

So, what does this mean for you as a leader? When it comes to motivation, speak with your team, find out what makes them tick, what their values are, what they want to master and what brings them meaning. Understanding these elements can help you build an environment of motivation within your team, driving the whole organisation to more success.

Leading In an Inspirational Way

Just because you've earned the title (or role) leader, doesn't mean you're automatically an inspirational leader. In fact, there are many (many) leaders in every industry and niche who aren't inspirational in the slightest. Instead, when you are an inspirational leader, you demonstrate your inspiration by your ability to drive your team and staff to reach greater levels of performance, better outcomes and more success.

Unfortunately, there are many senior leaders, even today, who still expect employees to follow them simply because of their title or their place in an organisation. While employees who value their paycheck will make

---

19   Pink, Daniel H. (2011) Drive: The Surprising Truth About What Motivates Us. Riverhead Books.

a show of 'following' their team and organisational leaders, that doesn't mean the leader inspires then to do their best work or contribute to the team as a whole.

Inspirational leadership starts with the skills we've already discussed—strategic thinking, planning and delivery, people management, communication and change management. But they don't stop there. An inspirational leader must also continue to inspire their teams and employees by utilising those skills with actionable efforts each and every day. In other words, they have to talk the talk *and* walk the walk.

In order to demonstrate inspirational leadership, let's start with a challenge that one company faced. This company, let's call it Company X, sold computer hardware, and one year, their orders for one particular product suddenly skyrocketed due to supply chain problems from overseas. This sudden need for more product coincided with the company's annual event, which would normally see most of their staff having two full days off of regular work.

Management felt that in order to ensure their customer's continued satisfaction, they needed to cancel the company event. But they also knew that many employees wouldn't like that decision. What can they do? Let's see if leading in an inspirational way can help them.

Actions That Inspire

As an inspirational leader, you don't just tell employees that you are committed to customer experience. You must demonstrate this commitment and passion in every meeting, presentation and customer interaction.

In the case of Company X, they were passionate about the customer experience, and felt that their staff having two days off work would impact on their ability to create that high-level experience. The good news here is that this feeling didn't come out of the blue (which could have felt like a money-grab rather than a true customer experience issue). Instead, the company's previous action had already shown their employees that they valued their customers. This was evident in their customer service KPIs, and in the high touch they provided at each customer interaction.

As a leader, your behaviour must inspire your team to value the same vision and behave in the same way.

Listening

To be an inspirational leader, just talking to your team about your vision is not enough. You need to listen, as well.

In order to inspire your team, to ensure they're involved and invested on a deep, internal level, you must listen to their thoughts, ideas and suggestions. And you must show them that you're listening. This involves setting up regular methods of receiving input–whether that's through meetings, reviews or some other way. But you also need to ensure you're available for informal input, which means engaging in 'water cooler' chats, or simply having an open-door policy.

In terms of Company X, the management didn't simply make a decision and expect everyone to adhere to it. Instead, they sought advice and input from employees from all levels about whether to cancel or reschedule the event. This allowed their employees to feel like they'd had a say in the final outcome.

> The more your team feels listened to, the more invested and included they'll feel.

The more your team feels listened to, the more invested and included they'll feel.

Once your team feels listened to, they're well on their way to feeling included. But to truly embed a sense of inclusion in your team, your action plan needs to also take these items into account.

Company X listened to and incorporated the ideas and input from their staff. This meant that in the end they didn't cancel the event. Instead, they held a smaller celebration that still created that positive morale boost but also allowed the company to meet their customers' needs.

Just like Company X, when you incorporate your team's ideas into the action plan your team will begin to feel truly involved and part of the process. When their ideas are included, they don't just feel heard, but also invested. And this inspires them to take the actions that will make their ideas (and your overall action plan) come to fruition. After all, no one wants to see their ideas fail.

Of course, you're not going to be able to implement every idea that your team presents, and that's OK. If you don't incorporate an idea, you simply need to explain why it doesn't work or why you aren't including it at this time. Your team just needs to feel a part of the process, even if it isn't the outcome, they would have chosen 100% of the time.

It's important to remember that no one is ever 100% supportive of a direction or vision they had no part in formulating. It's the action of creating the plan, generating and implementing ideas, that leads to a feeling of inclusion.

Integrity and Trust

To be an inspirational leader, vision and passion are a must. However, neither of these elements will matter in the slightest if your team doesn't also trust you.

In order to feel inspired, your team must wholeheartedly believe in your integrity. They need to see it in the decisions you make and actions you take each and every day. They need to know that you're going to tell the truth, that you're going to do what you say and say what you do and, most importantly, that you're always doing to do the right thing. Who you are as a person is as important as the direction you provide? People look up to a person who tells the truth, tries to do the right things, lives a principled life and does their best.

Giving People What They Want

As a leader, you can't always be a people pleaser—and you can't always give your team members exactly what they want. Certainly, your life would be easier if you could give pay raises and bonuses despite profits. Or could reward people with extra time off despite customer demands. That simply isn't feasible. But what you can do, and what an inspirational leader does, is give people what they want within their capabilities.

As an inspirational leader, you will understand what you *can* do to inspire your team. This might be praise, internal or even external recognition and other kinds of rewards. It might be as small (but important) as saying thank you for a job well done or speaking to a team member about the wonderful contribution they've been making to the organisation as a whole. Giving people what they want (and often they don't realise it is what they want) is vital if you want to be seen as an inspirational leader.

It's important to keep in mind that while you can't give a pay raise if the organisation hasn't met its profit goals, your team must believe that you would. They need to believe that you would (and will) share the monetary rewards if (and when) the organisation is doing well. (And when the company does well you have to put your money where your mouth is.)

The inspirational leader also understands that. They also understand that while money is a motivator, so are praise, recognition, rewards, saying thank you and noticing individual contribution. Speaking directly to a contributing employee about the value their work provides for the organisation is a key source of inspiration for the recipient.

Benefits of Inspirational Leadership

The quality of the leadership within your organisation is one of the main factors that will determine your success. But the success of your organisation is just one of the many benefits of inspirational leadership. And when it comes to your people, it's almost one of the least important.

So, what are the benefits of inspirational leadership?

Empower Others

Inspirational leaders empower their team. They give them the path and process to embrace passion in their work and to envision goals that support that passion. And then they work with them to create an action plan so they can better reach their goals.

Inspirational leaders invest in their team. They allocate time and resources to develop the talents of those around them and are happy to mentor (and help find mentors) as well. Sometimes this means reaching out to each employee in order to understand what's needed to bring out their best in them, and sometimes it's about being open to those conversations in a more informal way. However, inspirational leaders understand that they need to spend time with each employee to truly understand what they need in order to make their work life better and advance their career.

A truly inspirational leader understands that they will thrive best by helping those around them thrive, too.

Retention

When a leader spends time engaging with their employees and understanding their needs, this individual attention creates a strong, professional bond between them. This bond is an excellent way to reduce employee turnover and increase employee retention.

From an organisational point of view, strong retention is a benefit because it's costly to replace and train employees. However, from a leader's point of view, it's a benefit because having a stable team enables you to have a greater deal of control and a higher capacity to achieve your vision and overarching goals.

Meeting goals

Both retention and a feeling of empowerment help teams to better meet and even exceed their goals. This is because a team that stays together is stronger than one that has to deal with constant upheaval. And when a team is empowered, they're better able to make and take decisions for the good of the team and the entire organisation.

Above and beyond these two benefits, inspirational leaders are also better able to help their teams (and therefore themselves) to meet ambitious goals. By aligning their work with the values of their team, they can encourage others to take on more than they might otherwise believe they can. And the leader's constant support helps the entire team to meet and accomplish those goals consistently.

Increased engagement

This ongoing support and encouragement, the innate ability to value, praise and reward and the ability to reach out and listen to their teams, means that inspirational leaders have high engagement with their teams and, even better, their teams are highly engaged.

When you have high engagement with your team you are able to communicate a clear sense of purpose and the continued appreciation of each individual and the value they bring to the team as a whole.

When your team is highly engaged, they're committed to the team and the organisation, and they're more willing to take action based on this purpose–action that will be to the benefit of the organisation as a whole.

Committed employees

Committed employees are a vital part of any organisation. Just as being firmly committed to any relationship brings value to that relationship, when your team is firmly committed to your organisation, they bring added value to that organisation. This comes in the form of determination to succeed, high productivity and an awareness and desire to produce high-quality work. In addition, committed employees show less absenteeism and lower turnover.

Inspirational leaders inspire. And they do this by modelling the actions they want to see in their employees and team members, including a strong work ethic and a high level of commitment.

Growth

An inspirational leader is constantly involved with the growth of the company and the ongoing development of employees. This puts them in good position to understand what is happening, and how to meet these challenges within the microcosm of their own team. On the other hand, when a leader is not intimately involved in the growth of the company, they can find themselves struggling to manage and inspire their team when the company does begin to grow.

Company growth, particularly rapid growth, puts pressure on the leader and the team. If you are practicing the elements that create an inspirational leader, you'll also already have in place the elements that will help you manage your team during this time of change. These are things like channelling good company culture, recognising and rewarding your team for jobs well done, keeping communication open and easy and modelling the behaviours and actions you expect from your team. Each of these will help you and your team embrace, and even leverage, growth and change for the benefit of everyone involved.

As an inspirational leader you have all the skills and elements you need to make the process of growing an easier and more beneficial experience for all your employees.

Flexing Your Inspirational Muscle

When your team isn't just engaged, or motivated but actually inspired, that's when you will see incredible breakthroughs. Inspired employees are more committed and empowered. They stick around and follow the action plan because they've been involved in creating it and they believe in the outcomes. Better yet, they are inspired to set ambitious goals that will drive them to better results every day.

As an inspirational leader, your job becomes simultaneously easier, because your team is a fantastic support for you and your job, and more rewarding, because you are meeting your vision each day. Better yet, you have the benefit of increased knowledge and insight from your engaged team, which means better ideas, more productivity and a stronger end result (despite this not being a motivating factor).

Part 2

Team-Aware (Lead Your Team)

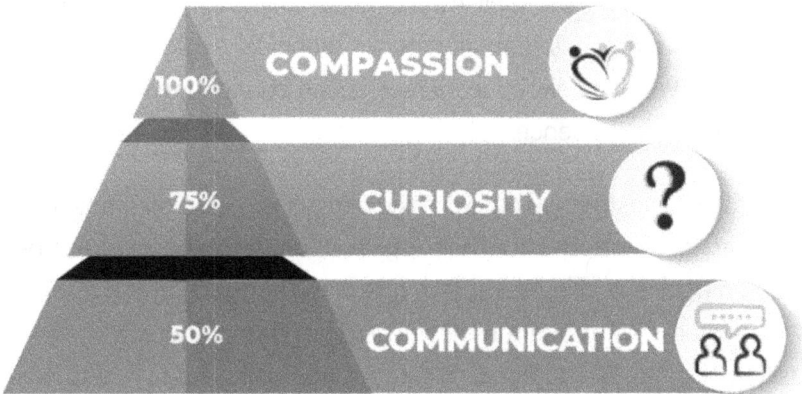

COMPASSION 100%

CURIOSITY 75%

COMMUNICATION 50%

Made For More definition: Being good, or the technical expert isn't going to be enough. We need skilled leaders who can connect and engage with their teams with influence.

''The challenge of leadership is to be strong, but not rude; Be kind, but not weak; Be bold, but not bully; Be thoughtful, but not lazy; Be humble, but not arrogant; have humour, but without folly.''

—Jim Rohn

As we've seen in Part 1 – Self-Aware (Lead Yourself), when it comes to leading your team, being an industry or technical expert isn't going to be enough. We need skilled leaders who can connect and engage with their teams with influence.

Leaders are constantly faced with the difficult decision of choosing the best management style for their organisation. And choosing the best leadership style is also essential in ensuring the success and retention of employees. When team members are led the wrong way, they can easily become discouraged, disorganised, unproductive and even disruptive. That's where the 'team-aware leader' comes into play.

A team-aware leader employs a people-oriented management style that builds relationships with employees. This style includes them in company operations by utilising and prioritising their soft skills instead of primarily their job-related skills.

A team-aware management style tends to energise employees because it makes them feel appreciated for the work they do. They feel they can make a difference in the company.

I love the story of Lakshmi Devi as a demonstration of true soft skills success. Lakshmi came from a small village called Somalapura, in Karnataka. When she was 18, she went to work in the city of Bengaluru as a tailor. At the time she had very little in the way of skills (soft or technical) as she hadn't been able to afford to continue on with her schooling. However, four years after she started her role, she became one of the youngest supervisors on the factory floor, overseeing the work of 80 tailors. And it all came down to soft skills.

Her employers had implemented a training program called P.A.C.E. (Personal Advancement and Career Enhancement)[20]. This was a program designed by Gap Inc. that trains women in soft skills, such as time management and communication. And for Laksmi, this was a major turning point in her life.

P.A.C.E. helped Lakshmi learn how to take and give responsibility, communicate effectively and make optimal use of her time. And it made her a better worker. As a supervisor, she implemented meetings in her line that improved productivity, created solutions for a disruptive floor and generated a greater feeling of camaraderie and respect while decreasing absenteeism. For herself, Lashmi has also seen better outcomes at home as a result of her training. Budgeting tactics now help her family to eat well and have enabled her younger sister to attend college. For the organisation, results have been equally stellar–

---

20   'P.A.C.E. - Empowering Women'. Gap Inc. Accessed at https://www.gapinc.com/en-us/values/sustainability/social/p-a-c-e-empowering-women.

nine months after the program completed, the company had an ROI of 250%[21].

And this is all down to soft skills.

The Three Key Pillars of Team Aware Leadership

The team-aware leadership style is centred around three key pillars:

- Communication – Being able to communicate with the purpose of connecting and influencing people and having the ability to handle tough conversations.
- Curiosity – A strong desire to know or learn more about those around you. This includes questioning, listening, and challenging.
- Compassion – The ability to put other people's needs ahead of your own. The desire to be kind show empathy to yourself and others. Understand the emotional intelligence ques to connect with people.

---

21   Adhvaryu, Achyuta , Garg, Lavanya , Kala, Namrata and Nyshadham, Anant. 'An Experiment in India Shows How Much Companies Have to Gain by Investing in Their Employees'. Harvard Business Review. 25 July 2017, updated 26 July 2017. Accessed at https://hbr.org/2017/07/an-experiment-in-india-shows-how-much-companies-have-to-gain-by-investing-in-their-employees.

Chapter 5

Communication

Made For More definition: The courage and skills to communicate with the purpose of connecting and influencing people, while having the ability to have tough conversations.

> '*Leadership is communicating to people their worth and their potential so clearly that they come to see it in themselves.*'
>
> —Stephen R Covey

Leaders are generally pretty good at conveying the 'what' to their team. That is what needs to be done and when. Where communication often fails is in conveying the 'why.' When you're asked 'why' by your employees, you don't want to be like the parent who says, 'because I say so'. Instead, you want to be able to clearly educate the reasons behind the actions. Effective communicators break down prohibitive information silos and build a communication strategy based on openness, the sharing of information and transparency.

Real influence starts by defining four things. The first is **'what'**. Your team needs to understand where your organisation stands and where it's headed. What specifically is the message at a high level? They need to understand the actions that are needed to get it to that desired place.

The second thing to communicate to your team is the **'why'.** The big picture 'why' helps them to understand the need for and importance of each of those actions. This style of communication also helps each team member to see the role they have to play in your organisation's overall success and creates forward momentum for everyone to move efficiently in the same direction.

Important to them personally, and the relevancy of why this is being communicated, and why now.

The third piece to communicate is the **'how'**, or the method by which what you're saying is going to be rolled out or implemented. This is where you explain the process.

Lastly, you want to communicate the **'what ifs**. This includes further details about what contingencies you have in place. This can also include references to any FAQs that may come up.

You should also be sure to celebrate the success of your big wins as this can yield big returns. In fact, according to organisational anthropologist and CEO Judith Glaser, celebrating success stimulates feelings of 'inclusion, innovation, appreciation, and collaboration' in the brain[22]. This paves the path for more creative thinking, a calmer work environment, increased focus and even a greater resilience to stress[23].

Speaking the right language

The first step to communicating well with your team is to understand the personality type of each of your employees. There are generally four broad types of employees that you will be communicating with on a frequent basis. There are your *Task Orientated* people, and the *People Orientated* people. Then there's the *Reserved* people, and then there's the *Outgoing* people. Each person within your team will fall into one of these board categories.

---

22   Glaser, Judith E. 'Celebration Time: A Cocktail Each Executive Should Know How to Mix.' Conversational Intelligence, Psychology Today. 28 December 2015. Accessed at https://www.psychologytoday.com/us/blog/conversational-intelligence/201512/celebration-time.
23   Ibid.

As you might imagine, *Task Orientated* people are more prone to making decisions based solely on logic and facts, while those who are people orientated make their decisions based on relationships and gut instinct. *People Orientated* people also tend to value what is 'good' over what is objectively best for the team while *Task Orientated* people will tend to value the objectives of the whole over individual needs.

Determining if your employees are 'Task' or 'People' orientated will make it exponentially easier to manage them. You may not know off the top of your head, so one great way to see who fits which type, is to simply watch how they react the next time someone disagrees with them. If they are emotional or upset, they are likely *People Orientated*. But if they can discuss the situation logically, looking for the best result for the team as a whole, then they are likely *Task Orientated*.

There is no one personality style that better than the other. Teams need all four styles, and varying degrees from moderate to extreme versions of each style. All four types of employees bring wonderful advantages to your team. And a good mix of all will ensure that you are able to leverage those benefits, without being overridden by one or the other. However, you do need to learn to communicate with them appropriately so that you're speaking the right language.

Task Orientated

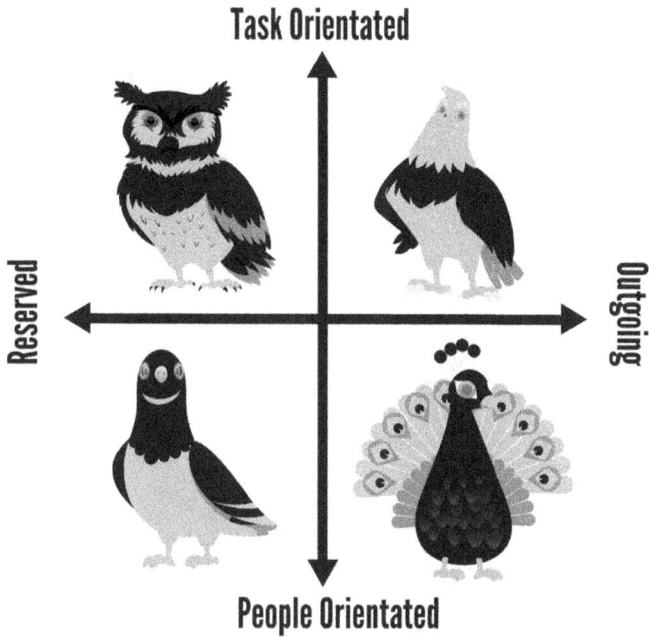

Reserved

Outgoing

People Orientated

The four personality types

A good way to think about each of the four personalities is as bird types.

Eagles – bold and decisive
Peacocks – showy and optimistic
Doves – peaceful and friendly
Owls – wise and logical

To identify each of the bird personalities within your team, here's some common traits.

Eagles and owls are more task orientated. They may:

• Be less disclosing of feelings
• Appear more reserved

- Display less facial expression
- Use less vocal inflection
- Use more facts and logic
- Be more task orientated, and
- Prefer working alone

Peacocks and Doves are more people orientated. They may:

- Express feelings more openly
- Appear more friendly
- Have more facial expression
- Use more vocal inflection
- Tell more stories
- Be more people orientated, and
- Prefer working with people.

Eagles and Peacocks are more outgoing. They may:

- Display more energy
- Move faster
- Gesture more
- Hold intense eye contact
- Lean forward when listening or talking
- Speak quicker (words per minute)
- Be more confrontational
- Decide quickly, and
- Demonstrate anger more quickly.

Owls and Doves are reserved. They may:

- Display less energy

- Move slower
- Gesture less
- Have less intense eye contact
- Lean backwards when listening or talking
- Speak slower (words per minute)
- Be less risk-orientated
- Be less confrontational
- Take time to decide, and
- Demonstrate anger less.

Looking at the individual traits

Eagles: Eagles tend to be strong willed and are individuals who value results, challenging opportunities and success

Peacocks: Peacocks tend to be enthusiastic and high-energy individuals who value quick action, collaboration and social recognition.

Doves: Doves tend to be patient individuals who are good listeners and value stability, collaboration and giving support.

Owls: Owls tend to be reserved analytical individuals who value accuracy, quality and orderly environments.

So, once you've identified your employees' personality types, adjust your management style to their way of working. This will require you to be more sensitive to the *People Orientated* people, actively listening and empathising, and more logical with the *Task Orientated* people, focusing on your talking points with supporting data and information.

It's important to remember that as the leader and communicator that you're adapting your natural style/language to your audience rather than expecting them to understand and speak your language.

Here are some tips when communicating with each style:

Your Language	Their Language	Focus on
Eagle	Dove	Focus more on feeling Get more personal Be supportive Slow your pace (word count) Listen more, listen better
	Peacock	Be open to their fun-loving side Adopt spontaneity Give them recognition Provide lots of freedom Focus on feelings
	Eagle	Don't come on too strong Be prepared with details Slow your pace Listen more, listen better.

Your Language	Their Language	Focus on
Peacock	Owl	De-emphasise feeling Be systematic Be well organised, detailed and factual Be more task orientated
	Dove	Slow your pace (word count) Listen more and listen better Don't come on too strong Be supportive
	Eagle	Be more task orientated De-emphasise feeling Plan your work Be well organised, Avoid a power struggle, focus on the task

Your Language	Their Language	Focus on
Dove	Owl	Be more task orientated De-emphasise feeling Be systematic Be well organised, detailed and factual
	Peacock	Focus on the big picture Say what you think Give them recognition Pick up the pace (word count)
	Eagle	Pick up the pace (word count) Demonstrate high energy Be more task orientated Be well organised, Say what you think

Your Language	Their Language	Focus on
Owl	Dove	Focus more on feeling Be supportive Provide structure Show interest in the human side Don't overdo facts and logic
	Peacock	Pick up the pace (word count) Get more personal Be open to their fun-loving side Give them recognition
	Eagle	Pick up the pace (word count) Demonstrate high energy Focus on the big picture Say what you think

Know what's most important to them

Adjusting your management and style to fit with your teams' varying personalities is just one element of communication. To really communicate well with a group of people, like your employees, you also need to understand what's important to them. Recognising their drivers, needs and wants helps you to communicate with them in a way that acknowledges those important factors and feels more authentic.

Demonstrate that they can trust you

Showing your team that they can trust you is a vital part of effective communication. In fact, research shows that when it comes to recommending their own organisation as a good place to work, employees were more likely to do so when they had high trust in their manager[24].

The research went on to say that there are three ways to build this trust:

1. Build positive relationships with your team.
2. Share your information and insights with others in your team, especially when it will benefit them.
3. Be consistent and keep your promises.

Quit taking things personally

Good communication is a two-way street—as a leader you need to be able to speak *and* listen. Often leaders will feel put out that their teams don't seem to listen well to them. But when we dig deeper, we find that it's the leaders themselves that haven't been listening. Instead, they've simply been 'listening to respond".

While directing your team is part of your role as a leader, it's just not effective communication. Many teams show reluctance to follow these

---

24   Folkman, Joseph. 'How Trust Affects Your Ability To Communicate And How To Fix It'. 7 April 2020. Forbes. Accessed at https://www.forbes.com/sites/joefolk-man/2020/04/07/how-trust-effects-your-ability-to-communicate-and-how-to-fix-it/?sh=32c1b523acae.

kind of Machiavellian directives. And when they don't it's easy to take it personally.

To properly communicate with your team, you need to remember to not take their reluctance to follow your directions too personally. Spend time identifying their personality type, determining what's important to them and winning over their trust, and you'll see things change for the better as you begin to build the foundation pieces to form a working relationship.

How To Have Courageous Conversations™

Our definition of a Courageous Conversations™ is an open honest and robust conversation that leads to a resolution, solution or progress.

Like it or not, the workplace is home to a number of difficult conversations. The research suggests that a tough conversation is avoided every seven minutes. It's not just the first seven minutes. But then it's delayed by fourteen minutes, then twenty-one, then avoided again until Friday 4:30pm, and, oops before you know if, it's been three months of avoiding a tough conversation.

As a leader who will have to discuss topics such as pay, benefits, performance (or underperformance) and even inappropriate behaviour it will be uncomfortable. However, having these difficult, but ultimately necessary, one-on-one conversations is what will make you a great leader.

While difficult conversations, or Courageous Conversations™ as we say, may not be fun, when you are able to navigate them successfully you will find that you've built stronger relationships with your employees and enabled better workplace outcomes and growth. This is because Courageous Conversations™ allow you to be in the fantastic position of providing guidance on workplace performance, behaviour and growth opportunities.

These honest, open, robust conversations let everyone know where they stand and how to best move forward to their next goal, and that knowledge is an excellent way to foster employee engagement and achieve fantastic organisational outcomes.

Create a culture of communication

Creating a culture of communication in the workplace is one of the best ways to have successful conversations with your employees. And a culture and environment of honest communication needs the following elements:

1. A foundation of trust and safety.

Good communication requires mutual trust and respect. You must ensure that employees feel comfortable sharing their thoughts. If they believe that their openness has the potential to carry professional, financial, social, physical or emotional risks, then they simply won't share with you.

But if they feel safe and believe that they won't be punished or ridiculed (or be at risk of losing their job), it gives them confidence to forge ahead and have those difficult conversations openly and honestly.

Foster a safe space for sensitive conversation by paying attention to the way you react to feedback and ideas. If your employees see you shutting others down, retaliating or otherwise reacting negatively when they come to you, they won't share with you in the future.

On the other hand, if you're open to input—even when it's not necessarily what you would want or choose—and employees see you listening, taking things on board and even implementing changes when it is the right thing to do, then they'll be much more likely to raise their voice when needed. And that means fresh insight, ideas, input and better outcomes.

2. Collaboration.

Now that you've built a foundation of trust, and have demonstrated your ability to listen and change, you'll be in a position to have difficult conversations. When having these difficult conversations, you need to focus on collaboration and to do that you should have two primary goals in mind at all times:

> First, educate the employee about the situation.
>
> Second, work to brainstorm ideas to solve the problem now or in the future.

Working collaboratively, you and your employee can bring together your individual thoughts on a situation. This will help flesh out any incomplete or half-formed ideas that could prove valuable if better conceptualised (but that will certainly fail if not). As part of this process, you need to be open to feedback about your own ideas, as well. And that includes accepting when you're wrong or unsure or when an employee's idea is better than your own.

3. Be responsive.

It's not enough to simply listen to your employees or collaborate on ideas. You also need to respond. And as part of that response, you need to demonstrate action. Your team need to see the impact of those difficult conversations. If you don't respond with action or answers, employees might believe that you conducted those difficult meetings just to check a box. And this will undercut any successes you might otherwise have from those and future conversations.

5 Steps to a Courageous Conversation™

Of course, when it comes time to sit down and actually have those courageous (but extremely important) conversations with a team member, what steps are you going to take? What is the best way to conduct that conversation and ensure that you keep your employee engaged and the conversation on track and helpful and designed to get you the outcomes you're looking for?

> "The standard you walk past, is the standard you accept".

When it's time for a Courageous Conversation™ just get on with it. After acknowledging the awkwardness, the best thing to do is make a start. Use direct language and get to the point quickly. But of course, you'll also want to think about your phrasing and word choice.

The reason you want to get on with it is, as Lieutenant-General, David Morrison Australian Chief of Army, has said, "The standard you walk past, is the standard you accept". The longer you avoid a performance or behavioural problem, the longer you're accepting that behaviour or problem.

Step 1 – Master Your Stories

One of the most common problems when it comes to a Courageous Conversation™ is the internal monologue that you tell yourself about a particular person or problem. This internal monologue stems from years of bias from childhood (your formative years, zero to eight years old) and includes things like, social and family norms, values, religious beliefs, what you were frequently told or learned through social interaction with your family, and social networks.

Mastering your stories takes a level of awareness—firstly of the internal monologue, or 'itty bitty shitty committee', and secondly of how to take control of the narrative by checking in to see if your stories are true. This can include things like:

- Refraining from labelling.
- Not assuming that your viewpoint is obvious.
- Being careful to be accurate and not exaggerate.
- Avoiding directives (i.e., don't tell others what to do).
- Refraining from blaming others for how you feel.
- Keeping it professional (and not personal).
- Trying to avoid judgments.

These kinds of statements or actions can trigger defensiveness and denial and will make it more difficult for you and your employee to have a productive conversation.

Instead, you need to be sure to:

- Use direct language.
- Keep your words clear.
- Use a neutral tone.
- Stay on task.
- Keep it professional.

In this way, you will only have to deal with the difficult topic itself, and not any other ancillary elements where your team member could take offense or have their feelings hurt.

Step 2: Go on a fact-finding mission

It's not enough to go on hearsay. Find your facts. What actually happened? What did you hear or see? If you are struggling with this, see step 1. Ask yourself, what are their stories?

You may believe you've gathered all the information you need already especially as, if you followed our suggestions above, you will have come into the conversation prepared. However, this doesn't remove the requirement to inquire about the reason for the problem from the other party. If you don't, you won't be participating in a conversation. You'll simply be giving a lecture.

You might be surprised to find that you don't actually know everything there is to know yet. Perhaps there was other vital information from the employee's perspective, or perhaps there are very different reasons underlying a problem than you expected. At the end of the day, it's the age-old problem of 'you don't know what you don't know'. Inquire first.

Step 3: Begin with the end in mind

We want to know where we're heading with this conversation. So, begin with the end in mind. You've gotten to the heart of the problem, so the next stage is to explore possible solutions. You need to ensure that your employee is aware of the seriousness of the situation and is committed to working collaboratively to find a solution. Brainstorm solutions together first, always ensuring that you're working with and supporting your employee in those efforts. Then be prepared to take action.

Sometimes you may need to create a formal action plan. And sometimes a more informal plan will work better. For either solution, plan to work together with your employee over the life of the plan.

What solution are you after?

What would be an ideal resolution or solution?

Step 4: Plan it out

Very little time is usually spent on planning out a Courageous Conversation™, yet this part is key. Do you have your stories in check? Do you have your facts from all parties involved? You know where you want the conversation to end—in a resolution or a solution?

Before you end the conversation, you need to recap. Review what was said and any action items you decided on. This kind of review and recap helps to cement the understanding and agreement in both of your minds and helps you to integrate the plan to move forward. This is also a good time to answer any lingering questions or clarify any ongoing confusion so that you are on the same page going forward into the future.

Step 5: Find the space

Now that you've completed steps one through four, the conversation is very much solution focused on the behaviour or problem rather than the person.

When it's time to actually have this conversation, find a space that is private and comfortable. Check in that you're in the right emotional space to have the conversation. Ask yourself, are you ready to sit next to the person rather than across from them? Are you willing to approach the problem in front of you rather than between you? And most importantly, are you ready to listen? Listen to understand rather than listen to respond.

Before you end the conversation, you need to recap. Review what was said and any action items you decided on. This kind of review and recap helps to cement the understanding and agreement in both of your minds and helps you to integrate the plan to move forward. This is also a good time to answer any lingering questions or clarify any ongoing confusion so that you are on the same page going forward into the future.

Generous Assumptions

Underpinning each of these steps is the Generous Assumption. This is the idea that most people want to do the right thing. Most people want to get along in the workplace. Most people want to do well in the work that they do. If you're having a Courageous Conversation™ usually there's been a communication gap, or an expectation gap, or even a capability gap. But allowing Generous Assumptions means that you come into all your Courageous Conversations™ with the right mindset.

How To Manage Virtual Teams with Excellent Communication

Another area that requires excellent leadership communication, and presents its own specific challenges, is in managing remote or virtual teams.

Even before the pandemic struck, businesses had begun to embrace the potential of a virtual team—where some or all team members live and work remotely. Virtual teams are an especially big draw for small businesses, home-based businesses or businesses that rely on freelancers or contractors. Implementing a virtual team reduces the overhead costs associated with a traditional office. And since you can hire from anywhere in Australia, or across the world, it also creates a much larger pool of potential (and often more affordable) applicants.

However, to have a productive virtual/remote/hybrid team you need to do more than just supply them with laptops and Microsoft Teams. Managers need to be fully across how to best manage, motivate and inspire their teams when they can't be with them all the time. And that comes down to excellent communication skills and processes.

Implement a shared collaboration tool

Different time zones are an opportunity to increase efficiency by enabling you to have a variety of staff who could potentially be working literally around the clock. However, this is also a major complication. Each member of your team needs to be across job responsibilities, deadlines and work delegation no matter where or when they are working.

This requires a robust and fluid form of communication that allows for updates and inputs from each member or your team and is easy for you to oversee and manage. And this can often be achieved through a collaboration tool.

There are many collaboration tools available, the first which often springs to mind is of course Asana. But there are many others. Or you may have a bespoke system built for your team or organisation. Whatever you choose you must ensure that you establish a well-calibrated set of rules about how your team will work together in the virtual environment and within that collaboration tool. And you must ensure that communication is easy and seamless with information transferring easily from one team member to another.

Expect the unexpected

Technology tools are just that... tools. They can never replace the human-to-human connection. And no matter how advanced it is, technology will fail you at some point–a poor internet connection, an unexpected software update or even a malfunction–it's vital that you have a back-up solution at the ready.

More importantly, you also need to have in place communications that foster the human connection. Video calls where you can see each other's facial expressions are a great way to do this. But having direct phone numbers that you can easily ring is also a good idea (and will help you remain in touch with your team even if there's a tech failure).

Hold each other accountable for communication

The expectation of communication needs to be built into your team culture from the very start. This means encouraging (even requiring) that the team speak directly to each other on projects or duties when they are collaborating. But it also means communicating on what they are working on even if it doesn't involve another team member specifically.

Fostering this network of communication builds a sense of trust among virtual teammates who understand who is working on what, when, and minimises any feelings of unfairness regarding workload or any ambiguity over assignments.

It's important to give this communication responsibility over to your team. As the leader you cannot be the only one through which communications are relayed. Not only is this much too taxing for you, but the flow of information will be bottlenecked, and the efficiency of the entire team impacted.

The Emotional Bank Account

When it comes to feedback, courageous leaders need to utilise what we call the emotional bank account. The emotional bank account is centred on John Gottman's work around maintaining successful relationships[25], and it posits that positive and negative feedback has an ideal ratio in order to be successful.

When it comes to leading our teams, we need to think about feedback all the time, with a focus on filling the 'in' column of our model. Every time you give a positive piece of feedback – that's specific and easily identified – you get a tick in the positive feedback column. Over time you can fill that column. And it's important that you do so, because when

<hr>

25 The Gottman Method. Accessed at https://www.gottman.com/about/the-gott-man-method/#:~:text=The%20goals%20of%20Gottman%20Method,the%20con-text%20of%20the%20relationship.

it comes to constructive (or negative) feedback, each piece is worth five positive pieces. In other words, each time you need to offer a piece of constructive feedback, it cancels out five positives.

This 1:5 ratio means that it's vital that you always keep adding to the positive column, because you don't know when the bad or constructive feedback will happen. So, to pre-empt this, you need to be continually filling the positive column. One of the perks is that you as the leader can see it come back as positive performance as well.

Maintain clarity

Of course, expecting team communication doesn't mean that you, as the leader, are off the hook. Part of your contribution is to ensure that you maintain clarity within communications at all times. The virtual team environment tends to blur all boundaries, including responsibilities. It's your job to clearly communicate to each team member so they are aware of what they need to do and when.

Be clear on expectations

George Bernard Shaw famously said, 'The single biggest problem in communication is the illusion that it has taken place." Being clear and explaining your expectations is paramount for both you and your team so neither one has a surprise.

Chapter 6

Curiosity

Made For More definition: A strong desire to know or learn something new, adapt an entrepreneurial mindset and make learning, studying, showing part of everyday life.

> 'Around here, we don't look backwards for very long. We keep moving forward opening up new doors, and doing new things, because we're curious… and curiosity keeps leading us down new paths.'
>
> —Walt Disney

Have you ever noticed how the best leaders also tend to be the most curious leaders? Great leaders simply aren't satisfied with what they know. They possess an insatiable curiosity for discovery and learning.

Since the dawn of time, the world has been shaped by leaders who understand that curiosity is the gateway to the future. Among many other things, curiosity helps frame vision, advance learning, fuel passion and drive innovation. Curiosity often inspires the courage to discuss the undiscussable, challenge current thinking, deviate from behaviours accepted as normal and to do what others previously thought impossible.

All great ideas and solutions begin from curiously asking the right questions. Thus, as a team-aware leader, you need to learn to ask the right questions.

You may know it as a growth mindset, or as simply asking the right questions but curiosity is an exceptional skill for leaders. Great leaders aren't satisfied with the status quo, or with the current state of any given situation and it's this curiosity that inspires the courage to see the future, challenge the current thinking, deviate from the norm and reach the impossible.

For the Courageous Leader™ this also means embracing opportunities to inspire curiosity in your teams and on an organisational level. Asking the 'right' questions is more than simply getting the right answers from your employees.

It's the tool for sparking creativity in their thinking and, ultimately, making those leaps to new discoveries.

What does curiosity look like as a leader in your team?

Curious leaders™ will likely be described as thirsty for knowledge—never satisfied with their existing knowledge, but always seeking to build on what they know. They will likely be the person that comes up with fresh, out-of-the-box ideas and, better yet, are driven to implement them. And they will likely be the question asker and the devil's advocate, looking to see what else they might be missing.

Curiosity brings energy and eagerness to learn which as a result turns into engagement when fostered and not quashed. It is courageous as it's often a quality that can involve risks. But it can also be harnessed, built up and even reinvigorated. After all, curiosity is not reserved for new employees or new businesses. Some of the most powerful, successful and long-standing businesses are those that value curiosity.

In 2004 an anonymous message was displayed on a billboard overlooking Highway 101, in the centre of tech-heavy Silicon Valley. The message read: '{first 10-digit prime found in consecutive digits of e}.com'. Those that could solve it got the answer of 7427466391.com. When they followed this link online, they were given another equation to solve. Those that managed to solve that next equation were then invited to submit their resume to Google.

This unusual approach to recruiting was designed to find those that possessed that special skill of curiosity (as well as intelligence).

Eric Schmidt, CEO of Google from 2001-2011 said, 'We run this company on questions, not answers.

Curiosity is a value that is at work in every conversation, every communication, every interchange and every innovation, whether that's in the boardroom or in the shared kitchen. Bringing that authentic curiosity opens up your business to incredible advantages.

Why is Curiosity Important in Leadership?

Smart leaders know curiosity is an important quality to foster in leadership that can result in agile, accomplished teams. In fact, being able to 'pivot' has long been considered a make-or-break character trait for organisations. And this has only been strengthened since the pandemic regardless of industry or company size.

Those who foster curiosity have been able to reap the benefits of increased creative thinking and problem solving, as well as greater collaborative approaches to problems on a team and organisational level. But the benefits continue.

There are three main elements and three sub elements for the Curious Leader™

Listening

Listening is an incredibly underutilised skill for leaders and leaders who are looking to improve their coaching capability. Listening helps to understand what's not being said. Listening as skill increases Emotional Intelligence (EQ) and created a deeper level of understanding, of both the problem and the person.

Questioning

Ask better questions, get better answers. Often leaders are in the position they are because they are technically great at a skill. To be a good curious leader is learning and understanding the best questions to get better answers.

Challenging

Challenging is a key part of the curious leader. Often leaders have an idea of what is right (or wrong). When leaders are curious and challenging, they develop a deeper understanding of individual drivers as well as the ability to experience and share different perspectives.

Listening + Challenging = Opportunity

When leaders are great listeners, and they can challenge thinking, the opportunity for what's next is limitless. Whether it's the individual they're coaching or as a group, opportunity lies in the 'what's next for you, for the team

Listening + Questioning = Understanding

Being able to listen and question what someone is say, and more importantly not saying (EQ) is incredibly important when it comes to understanding the needs of the individual or group, and also where to take the next steps as a leader who coaches.

Questioning + Challenging = Possibility

When questioning and challenging intersect, there is a limitless possibility to what is available Whether it's an individual's performance and capability, or a team taking on a whole new challenge. Being able to challenge and question without judgement or an agenda unlocks limitless possibilities.

Benefits of Curiosity in Leadership

First, curiosity increases perseverance–a vital element of a strong team and a strong leader particularly in challenging times. Research[26] shows that simply describing a day when you felt curious boosts your mental and physical energy by 20%, helping you to have the capacity to do more and be more.

Second, curiosity enhances intelligence. In one study[27], highly curious children were able to improve their IQ scores by 12 points more than the least curious children.

Third, curiosity drives us towards deeper engagement, superior performance and higher goal achievement. This was demonstrated in another study[28] where curious psychology students got higher grades and took on more course work than their counterparts.

As a leader and a team, these traits–perseverance, intelligence and deeper engagement, performance and achievement–are without a

---

26   Kashdan, Todd B., Disabato, David J., Goodman, Fallon R. and Naughton, Carl . 'The Five Dimensions of Curiosity. How are you curious?' Harvard Business Review Magazine. September–October 2018. Accessed at https://hbr.org/2018/09/the-five-dimensions-of-curiosity.

27   Ibid.

28   Ibid.

doubt highly desirable. But they also have knock-on effects within the team environment.

In fact, Francesca Gino, in research for *Harvard Business Review* discovered that there were 'fewer decision-making errors, more innovation and reduced group conflict, more open communication and better team performance' when curiosity was actively cultivated in the workplace[29].

In this study, 200 employees from diverse industries were sent morning text messages either to encourage curiosity (such as 'What is one topic or activity you are curious about today?' Or 'Please make sure you ask a few "why questions" as you engage in your work throughout the day.') and another group to prompt reflection but not curiosity (such as 'What is one topic or activity you'll engage in today?' or 'What is one thing you usually work on or do that you'll also complete today?').

After receiving their assigned text messages twice, a week for four weeks those who'd had their curiosity piqued demonstrated higher innovative behaviours at work and reported making more constructive suggestions and solutions for important organisational issues. This is just one of many examples of studies that have shown that curiosity is more important than first thought when it comes to organisational performance and can be a vital tool to incorporate into one's leadership toolkit.

Fostering curiosity as a leadership tool can reduce defensiveness as well as give better communication between groups when working towards a common goal. And teams with innate or cultivated curiosity had less of a confirmation bias.

---

29   Gino, Francesca. 'The Business Case for Curiosity.' Harvard Business Review Magazine. September–October 2018. Accessed at https://hbr.org/2018/09/the-business-case-for-curiosity.

Confirmation bias is where we seek to see or interpret evidence in a way that supports what we already believe or do—essentially our organisational stereotypes[30]. However, when a team's curiosity is sparked, they are more likely to engage in creative thinking to get better, newer or more innovative answers. They're also more likely to communicate with each other more effectively as they work together to satisfy that quest for knowledge and answers.

Ultimately, what does that mean for leadership?

Inspiring curious thinking can bring up limiting constructs you as a leader, and your team more generally, might not even realise you have. It creates greater space, capacity and courage to engage in difficult conversations and tackle harder problems. It leads to more innovative solutions and brings teams together with more cohesion. Most importantly, because curiosity values fresh ideas and perspectives, it lets your employees know their ideas are not only valued but also encouraged.

How Curiosity Can Transform Your Business or Organisation

Curiosity, or merely asking questions, could be the key to transforming your business. Just a few small changes within your team and the way you lead and manage your team could lead to an increase in curiosity, regardless of the industry or niche you operate in. And that increase in curiosity can improve your company overall.

---

30   Nickerson, Raymond S. 'Confirmation Bias: A Ubiquitous Phenomenon in Many Guises.' Review of General Psychology. June 1998. Accessed at https://journals. sagepub.com/doi/10.1037/1089-2680.2.2.175.

Benefits of Curiosity to Your Business or Organisation

- **Better communication and decreased conflict.** Curiosity leads to better, more positive communication within business teams. And good communication reduces group conflict, creating a better team performance overall.

- **Improved growth mindset.** Curious teams relish in both personal growth and shared learning leading to a culture that embraces the growth mindset.

- **Higher emotional wellbeing.** Surveys show that teams who were encouraged to give honest feedback, engage with mutual respect and have more personal openness teams were 80% more likely to report higher emotional well-being[31].

- **Reduces decision-making errors.** Decision making errors in business are costly[32]. Great leaders are known to be decisive but can often find themselves in challenging positions as they manage emotion and reason in decision making. They can also struggle under the fear of making an error—often with heavy costs, negative reactions and even push back from staff to consider. By inspiring curiosity in an organisation, leaders made fewer decision-making errors, because curious minds are more likely to generate more alternatives and not fall back on what we think we already know.

- **Encourages innovation.** Curiosity can transform your business by encouraging more innovative options and helping you and your team be more open to ideas in general.

---

31 Middleton, Tracy. 'The importance of teamwork (as proven by science)'. Atlassian. 25 January 2022. Accessed at https://www.atlassian.com/blog/teamwork/the-importance-of-teamwork.

32 Milkman, Katherine L., Chugh, Dolly and Bazerman, Max H. 'How Can Decision Making Be Improved?' 2008. Harvard Business School. Accessed at https://www.hbs.edu/ris/Publication%20Files/08-102_1670bc7e-dc3c-49c8-bc5f-1eba2e78e335.pdf.

Innovation isn't just about the product your business makes or the service you offer. It's also about how you run your business, how you adapt and grow. Having a culture driven towards curiosity can increase innovation that may give your business a competitive advantage, increase sales and reduce employee turnover. And although you might not know where the next innovation will come from, having a curious approach in your leadership or an environment that is open to ideas is when this can flourish.

- **Lead with humility.** On an individual level, as a leader, flexing your curiosity muscle may be another great opportunity for you to lead with humanity. Adding curiosity to some of the more traditional 'traits for successful leadership' (often cited as humility, resilience, empathy, intuition, gratitude and self-confidence[33]), will take you from being a good leader to an exceptional leader.

Challenges to Curiosity

Despite understanding all the benefits, there are often challenges to curiosity within the corporate or business environment. Sometimes new ideas and enthusiastic out-of-the-box thinking are quashed because of confirmation bias (as discussed above). We like to stick with what we know and where we feel comfortable.

Other times this new thinking might be rejected because of insecurity or fear. As leaders it's our job to control risk within our teams and organisation. But new ideas challenge what we know to be safe, increasing our vulnerability to risks in the future. We may also come up

---

33   Ashok, Asokan. 'Leading With Humanity: Six Traits For Successful Leadership'. Forbes. Aug 4, 2020. Accessed at https://www.forbes.com/sites/forbestech-council/2020/08/04/leading-with-humanity-six-traits-for-successful-leader-ship/?sh=358a2434427e.

against the problem of ego. New ideas challenge what we've been doing and, from one perspective, our correctness in taking that previous. As leaders we might see this as having to prove ourselves once again.

Finally, as we get older, we'll struggle more to keep the curiosity in our lives. Curiosity is an innate skill of the young (think of the small child who wants to know the details of every tiny element of life, if you have a three-year-old, you'll know). However, this is a skill that wanes over time, not because we become less curious (studies show that we remain curious even into old age), but because we have less mental agility to embrace that curiosity[34].

Because of these challenges, when a leader is keen and eager to become a successful *and curious* leader, they can sometimes struggle to implement the necessary curiosity trait. But being able (or having the skill set) to ask the right questions to get the information you need is a vital part of ensuring that your leadership intentions are marrying up with your leadership behaviours.

In fact, only 20% of managers and leaders ever ask for reverse feedback from their team[35]. That means 80% don't. This is unacceptable for a curious leader, as asking questions is the all-important first step to obtaining the benefits that can arise from embracing curiosity in yourself and your team. Yet, they are often held back by fear.

A fear mindset is something that will hinder you as a leader, and an organisation's ability to become curious (and reap the resulting rewards). Having toxic culture or trust issues can be at play when

---

34 Stokoe R. 'Curiosity, a Condition for Learning'. Questia.com. 2012. Available from: https://www.questia.com/library/journal/1P3-3009007551/curiosity-a-condition-for-learning.

35 van Hooydonk, Stefaan. 'The Curious Leader: Leadership Lessons to Cultivate Curiosity'. *Mercuri Urval*. 2020. Accessed at https://www.mercuriurval.com/en-au/institute/insights/belgium/the-case-for-curiosity/.

attempting to get to the crux of curiosity. There is often a disparity between what employees and management think about the openness of conversion that curiosity brings as a communication style. It's a leader's role to ensure there is a culture of openness and acceptance to curiosity and curiosity-based conversations. Employees also need to feel psychologically safe to partake in those conversations. A fear mindset will ensure that they never do.

How to Cultivate Curiosity as a Leader and a Team

Despite the challenges that face us as leaders in creating an ecosystem of curiosity and questioning, and the resulting ideas and innovation, it's important that we make the changes needed to cultivate that curiosity.

Inspiring curiosity within your team is about creating a learning environment where everyone is involved in transactional learning from each other's experiences, knowledge, and ideas. But without a top-down approach to instilling a curiosity culture, organisations may miss out. You, as the leader, are the first and best role model for this new behaviour. In fact, there is a direct correlation between how intensely you learn and how intensely your team models that behaviour. In other words, the more that you engage in curious learning, the more your team will as well[36].

So how can you inspire curiosity within yourself as a leader? How do you build your own inquisitive mind? And how do you demonstrate that focus to your team?

1. **Learn, Study, Read (LSR).** Learn, study, and read about people who are doing what you're doing, or who are inspiring you in other industries entirely. Find out how they became great, how they continue to stay great and how they overcame

---

36   Ibid.

any failures (because everyone fails, it's how we overcome them that matters).

2. **Take your time.** When you're presented with a problem, take your time to think about it before moving forward with a solution. In our busy world, thinking time is at a premium. But the best ideas come to us when we're not pushing for a solution, but simply puzzling out different ways of responding. We'll find we see new angles, new possibilities and, ultimately, a new answer.

3. **Ask 'why'.** Just because you've always done something one way, doesn't mean it's the right way. Ask 'why' when presented with a well-used solution or well-trod path. Make it a habit of understanding why you are doing something before you do it and encourage your team to do the same. Questions are the best way to improve collaboration and results.

4. **Say less, listen more.** No matter the situation, try to prioritise listening to others' thoughts and ideas over sharing your own. Hearing these ideas will help you to expand your own thinking, giving you new perspectives and new ways to grapple with problems. It will even give you an opportunity to ask questions that might generate innovative ideas in yourself and others.

5. **Talk to your junior team members.** As leaders, particularly senior leaders, you might find yourself spending the majority of our time talking to colleagues who are at a similar stage as ourselves. To foster curiosity, talk to your junior colleagues. Ask them what they're doing in their free time, what they're interested in and what they're learning about. It's refreshing, it's illuminating and it's a reminder that we have a choice about whether to be curious or not in our own lives.

Remember, it's your choice as a leader whether to choose to embrace the gamut of beneficial effects born from curiosity or suffocate its favourable flow. But if you choose the latter, you might be sentencing yourself to a limited lifespan in your career.

According to Gartner TalentNeuron™ data analysis on millions of job postings, 'the number of skills required for a single job is increasing by 10% each year over year, and over 30% of the skills needed three years ago will soon be irrelevant'[37].

We must rely on our intrinsic human qualities, one of which is curiosity, to succeed. It is the role of the leader to lead the motivation and engagement required to sustain and maximise innovative thinking– with curiosity being the driver. Moreover, strategic moves to set up an ecosystem pro-curiosity is the key to letting its magic flow.

What Does Curiosity Sound Like?

Ultimately curiosity is a communication skill, and a vital one for any modern organisation where the challenges to keep up are high. Luckily you know curiosity well, even if you don't remember. After all, it was a major part of your childhood toolkit.

Implementing 'the sound of curiosity' is sometimes as easy as putting on your 'curiosity lens' and getting comfortable with humility. It sounds like a positive open tone of voice that conveys a desire to learn, an inquisitiveness, but rather than judgement or ego. Sometimes it sounds like an open-ended question that may come with several clarification questions and much back and forth (we are aiming for a curious conversation, not just a curious question).

When implementing curiosity into your organisation it is much like many other soft skills that comes through change–it takes time and practice

37   Baker, Mary. 'Stop Training Employees in Skills They'll Never Use'. *Gartner.* 24 September 2020. Accessed at https://www.gartner.com/smarterwithgartner/ stop-training-employees-in-skills-theyll-never-use.

to get right. As a leader, you may have to put aside the fact you are the one used to giving the answers and become comfortable with admitting you don't know everything.

When you bring curiosity into your team, you will find that you're now discovering what your team needs, rather than just guessing, and this is a sure-fire way to create engagement, bring value and inspire action. As a bonus, you might even find it freeing.

Practicing Curiosity in Leadership

- DO Remember to ask questions that inspire curiosity from a place of learning.
- DO role model conversations with your team, let go of being the one that has to give the answers and embrace asking questions, pursue other people's perspectives and share your ideas in conversation.
- DO use open-ended questions ('why', 'how', 'what if' questions) alongside an open tone of voice, an open mind and open body language.
- DO ask clarifying questions
- DO connect with your team. Lead the way in connection, while inspiring curiosity, enthusiasm and inspiration from your team.
- DO celebrate in shared goals and wins.
- DO Implement other 'soft skill' leadership traits such as empathy and humility plus a generous helping of emotional intelligence to 'read the room' when it comes to asking curious questions.
- DO remember to practice - Often the most courageous conversations™ we have are new and challenging.

- DO rephrase the question in a curious slant. For example, change 'What is one topic or activity you'll engage in today?' to 'What is one topic or activity you are curious about today?'
- DO remember you (as a leader) are always learning and trying to move away from your own cognitive biases that we (as humans) tend to fall back on.
- DO keep asking questions.
- DON'T assume.
- DON'T leave anyone out. Inclusivity is important to build trust.
- DON'T judge or find fault. The team or person you are communicating with must not feel at fault or judged as this will only elicit a defensive response.

Flexing Your Curiosity Muscle

You've moved away from a fear-based mindset where new solutions appear risky, expensive and inefficient. You are convinced by the research that curiosity is the way forward when it comes to pushing you out of your normal 'comfort zone' to a place where more creative solutions are accessible. You recognise that curiosity in business is an elite tool to unlock new perspectives, create more engagement, energise and deliver better team performance leading to better financial outcomes. Now, it's time to flex your curiosity muscle.

Curiosity is a trait you can encourage on a personal level as well as implement on an organisational level. Start by asking yourself some curious questions or challenge yourself on 'How can I be more curious today?' Or when planning your week think about what opportunities you must implement your new curiosity strategies. Plan to ask curious questions during your team catch ups or just while you are grabbing your morning coffee.

Start out by leaving judgment at the door and stepping into your open mind. Use open ended questions using 'why', 'how' and 'what if'. And show genuine interest to the genuine answers that you will receive.

Act as a role model to your team on how to be curious and like most things in leadership realise that it may not necessarily be smooth sailing. It is your job as a leader to rock the boat and reap all the benefits that cultivating curiosity can bring to you, your team and your organisation.

Chapter 7

Compassion

Made For More definition: Compassion is the desire to be kind and show empathy to yourselves and to others, recognising that every team member is a significant and essential thread in the entire organisation.'

'The best leaders blend
courage with compassion.'

—Robin Sharma

You're familiar with sympathy and empathy. But a basic human quality that we learn as children may be the key to moving us through emotionally charged sympathy and empathy. And that key is compassion.

While it's true that as a leader you need to be emotionally intelligent and have the ability to empathise with your team as a whole as well as with individual members, it's compassion that allows you to take action on those empathetic emotions. It allows you to both identify with, but also lead through, empathy and sympathy, to drive outcomes that are beneficial for your team members, your team and the entire organisation.

If you're unable to move through challenging moments that arrive due to your empathy, you are at risk of developing 'empathy fatigue' (or sometimes even called 'compassion fatigue'). Empathy fatigue happens when you rely too heavily on identifying with the emotions as opposed to identifying and then moving through them. And it results in traumatic stress and burnout that can create physical and mental exhaustion because your ability to cope with your everyday environment has been severely depleted[38]. That's no way to live... or to lead.

---

38 Cocker, F., Joss, Nerida. 'Compassion Fatigue among Healthcare, Emergency and Community Service Workers: A Systematic Review'. International Journal of Environmental Research and Public Health. June 2016. Accessed at https://www.ncbi.nlm.nih.gov/pmc/articles/PMC4924075/.

Instead, we must ensure that we don't rest in compassion, but instead focus on leading with compassion.

The benefits of compassion in leadership have long been understood. They include increased collaboration and trust levels, enhanced loyalty and greater employee engagement[39]. Better yet, compassionate leaders are perceived as stronger and more competent[40].

Compassionate leaders have been well and truly tested in recent years as the pandemic has tightened its grip on organisational and employee wellbeing.

> We must ensure that we don't rest in compassion, but instead focus on leading with compassion.

But there's never been a more important time to focus on compassionate leadership. After all, leaders that lead with compassion have happier and more harmonious teams. More cohesive teams also tend to deliver better results—with a positive impact on both the individual and for the business as a whole. But we must continue to take care. The pandemic has seen a necessary rise of interest in employee wellbeing. As part of that leaders may be at risk of taking the brunt of the emotional fallout that goes alongside. But could leading with compassion be your tool to dodge empathy burnout?

It's true that good leadership requires dedication to lead with humanity and authenticity. By being intentionally compassionate, you can

---

39 Hougaard, Rasmus, Carter, Jacqueline and Hobson, Nick. 'Compassionate Leadership is Necessary--but Not Sufficient.' *Harvard Business Review.* 4 December 2020. Accessed at https://hbr.org/2020/12/compassionate-leadership-is-necessary-but-not-sufficient.

40 Ibid.

communicate your true and genuine willingness to help others. Even in challenging times that at first may appear as a hurdle, it's your sincerity that will connect you with an individual and your drive to not only identify with, but also push for change that can propel this into a positive leadership experience. These elite traits are considered exceptional qualities and may take you from being a good leader to an exceptional leader.

Let's learn more.

The Compassion Continuum: Sympathy, Empathy and Compassion

Sympathy

Where does compassion start? As a child navigating the world, your understanding of compassion usually starts with a realisation or recognition that other people suffer or feel things, just like you do. This could happen in a number of ways. For example, it may be seeing someone who has lost a teddy. You feel sorry for that child—and that feeling becomes your first encounter with sympathy. Or at least the first moment you recognise it as a feeling.

Empathy

Then the more you think about, and perhaps put yourself in that child's shoes, the more you begin to take on that emotion yourself. Suddenly, you don't feel sorry for the other child. You feel that emotion as if you were the one who had lost that favoured toy. This response is empathy.

Within empathy itself, there are three different levels:

1. Cognitive empathy—which is being aware of another person's emotional state

2. Emotional empathy—which is engaging and sharing in those emotions

3. Compassionate empathy—which is taking action to support other people.[41]

Compassion

Sympathy and empathy, though kissing cousins of compassion, aren't, in fact, the same thing. Compassion arises from empathy—particularly from compassionate empathy. Compassion comes when you wish for those sad or hard feelings to dissipate—in other words, when you want that person to feel better. And, eventually, that motivates you to take action to relieve that suffering.

The difference driving the shift in this continuum (from pity to sympathy to empathy to compassion) is the motivation to act. There is a connection between understanding another person's experience and a willingness to act, which drives the resulting compassion. It becomes more than just a feeling but a supportive and intentional action. Ultimately, when compassion is your driving force you are willing to do something to help solve a problem.

Even as young children we have the ability to move through the continuum from pity to compassion. So, in reality, we have been practising compassion our whole lives. Although we may be more inclined to exercise it more readily at different times (for example when we are well rested or feel like we have the mental capacity) making

---

41 'Empathy at Work: Developing Skills to Understand Other People'. *Mind Tools.* Accessed at https://www.mindtools.com/pages/article/EmpathyatWork.htm#:~:-text=Cognitive%20empathy%20is%20being%20aware,action%20to%20sup-port%20other%20people.

compassion is an intentional choice. And it's one that pays off when it comes to being an exceptional leader, particularly if you are interested in fostering genuine connection which in turn can be a huge benefit to you and your organisation.

Beware of Empathy Paralysis

We touched a bit on empathy fatigue in the beginning of this chapter. But empathy fatigue is only the first step in a bigger problem–empathy paralysis.

Although empathy is cited as one of the Six Traits For Successful Leadership[42] (along with humility, resilience, intuition, gratitude and self-confidence) some leaders who might be experiencing empathy burnout may find it difficult to push through. This is what we call paralysing empathy–and it's essentially exactly as the name indicates. It is empathy that paralyses you from taking action.

As leaders when we suffer from empathy paralysis, we are unable to move past the feelings to the action. This stops us from tackling a more intentional, motivated, compassionate approach in our leadership. Having the ability to identify and feel someone's suffering may lead us to a deeper connection with that person. But if we can't act on it, then it can cloud our decision-making accuracy and our judgement as a leader.

Paul Bloom, author of Against Empathy and Professor of Cognitive Science and Psychology at Yale University, conducted a study to see if empathy can distort judgement. Two groups were asked to listen to a recording of a terminally ill child describing his pain. Group one was instructed to identify and feel for the child. On the other hand, group

---

42   Ashok, Asokan. 'Leading with Humanity: Six Traits for Successful Leadership.' *Forbes.* 4 August 2020. Accessed at https://www.forbes.com/sites/forbestech-council/2020/08/04/leading-with-humanity-six-traits-for-successful-leader-ship/?sh=1cb36159427e.

two was asked to listen objectively and not emotionally engage. Then each person was asked to decide if the child should be moved up a medically prioritised treatment list, giving benefits to that child, but potentially putting others more at risk.

The results showed that those that were emotionally connected to the child were more likely to move the child up the list even against professional medical opinions (three quarters of the group). However, of those that objectively listened to the child, only a third of the group made the same decision.

There are certainly benefits to taking action related to empathy. But there also seems to be a skill in having the right amount of empathy. This is the level that allows you to move through the empathy to the magic space where compassionate leadership shines. Being intentional with your shift to compassion is a proactive leadership choice that can benefit you (in terms of the load you bear). But it is also highly beneficial to your team, giving them an open supportive space to voice concerns, challenges, and problems, as well as a psychologically safe space to sit with potential issues knowing that actionable solutions are at hand.

Compassion to Others–A Welcome Shift

The term burnout was first coined in the 1970s, but since then it has become more and more well-known and widespread. This has only been exacerbated since the pandemic which caused both the recognition of the term itself, and the number of people who suffer from burnout's effects, to rise. High ideals combined with severe stress is leaving more and more people in this space–exhausted, listless, unable to cope, burned out. In fact, it's more common today, than ever before with the World Health Organisation recognising it as an occupational health issue in 2019[43]. And a study from Indeed found more than half of workers surveyed felt burnt out and two-thirds of those felt it had gotten worse since the onset of the pandemic[44].

On a societal level there has been a shake up as to what people want, what they value, and what they are willing to commit to in their working lives. In a post-pandemic world, the drive for 'balance' is more present than ever and doesn't discriminate according to industry or level. Millions of people are making career changes or giving up their roles in the search for something new, from frontline workers to senior executives.

Compassionately Leading Your Team

When it's done well, your compassionate leadership can optimise your team performance as you shift your focus from empathy to compassion. And this is because your team feels the absence of judgement (the same judgement that is prevalent in so many work environments today). And when they don't feel judged–but instead feel safe, understood and secure, their stress is lowered, and so is their opportunity for burnout. It also has a major beneficial effect on staff retention.

To compete, businesses need to look at staff retention as a major priority in a modern business world. It's more than the promises of pay rises or an employee gym membership that have people staying in their jobs. It's an artful intentional plan to create a solid culture, co-creative workplace and having leaders at the helm that genuinely care.[45]

---

43   Doniger, Alicia. 'The future of work is here, employee burnout needs to go'. CNBC. 23 September 2021. Accessed at https://www.cnbc.com/2021/09/23/the-future-of-work-is-here-employee-burnout-needs-to-go.html.

44   Threlkeld, Kristy. 'Employee Burnout Report: COVID-19's Impact and 3 Strategies to Curb It. Indeed. 11 March 2021. Accessed at https://www.indeed.com/lead/preventing-employee-burnout-report.

45   Ron Carucci, 'To Retain Employees, Give Them a Sense of Purpose and Community' https://hbr.org/2021/10/to-retain-employees-give-them-a-sense-of-purpose-and-community

As well as building trust, connection, collaboration and a cohesive team environment, it seems that adding compassion to your leadership toolkit is a valid and authentic way to tackle employee retention. It's important to remember that moving toward cultivating compassion in the workplace, or at least into your own leadership style, isn't being anti-empathy or against human connection. If anything, it allows you to sidestep the emotional element, freeing you to be better placed to offer support and/or solution when trouble arises.

Remember, compassion, like many of the concepts we discuss in courageous leadership, may not be enough alone to become an exceptional leader. Even when you master the art of compassion, it is the role of a great leader to combine that with wise, competent and effective leadership to get the results[46], a term that has been coined 'wise compassion'.

Adding (wise) compassion to your leadership style can help you be more human even when you have to tackle the more difficult jobs of leadership. This could include courageous conversions, hard decision making and giving feedback you may not want to give. But having and displaying compassion is known to correlate to better outcomes for your team and your organisation.[47]

How to demonstrate and practice compassion

Of course, nailing these more 'human traits' in leadership can seem difficult to both learn and measure, particularly when it comes to getting the balance right. You may be wondering if you can 'learn' compassion.

46   Hougaard, Rasmus, Carter, Jacqueline, Hobson, Nick. 'Compassionate Leadership Is Necessary — but Not Sufficient'. *Harvard Business Review.* 4 December 2020. Accessed at https://hbr.org/2020/12/compassionate-leadership-is-necessary-but-not-sufficient.
47   'Compassionate Leadership Is Necessary'. HBR.

And, equally, important, if you can learn to utilise it without slipping over the edge into fatigue or, worse, paralysis.

Like many of the traits we value in a great leader, compassion can and should be practised daily, with yourself and within your team. Role modelling compassion in your team can help 'filter down' this intrinsic trait creating a considerable ripple effect and ultimately making space for others to gain compassion's benefits. Cultivating compassion can only be a beneficial exercise for creating community within your team.

- **Make the shift from 'I' to 'we':** When your conversations revolve around 'I' statements that consist mostly of your own perspective, you can be missing out on valuable opportunities to create genuine connection and compassion. This automatically makes you more open-minded and creates more genuine conversion.

- **Practice gratitude:** Valuing a team member's work can do great things for employee loyalty and drive. Being gracious, saying thank you or demonstrating to someone that you care shows that you are a compassionate leader and that their contribution is valued.

- **Collaborate:** Creating a compassionate culture has multiple benefits in a team setting such as increased communication, more trust, and engagement through working towards shared goals. At the end of the day, showing the team that you care can result in greater influence and better results.

- **Understand your impact:** Daily acts of compassion and creating compassionate environments (that foster engaged employees) may be more motivating than employee wellbeing packages and your approach to leadership can have knock on effects on your employees' wellbeing.[48]

- **Start today:** If you're reading this chapter and asking yourself if you could be a more compassionate leader, the chances are you may be missing out on a valuable method of creating a crucial connection with your team.

Self-Compassion for Better Leadership

The benefits of compassion are also applicable to yourself as a leader, and as a human. Self-introspection and inwardly practising compassion can lead to more constructive outcomes for you which can have a flow on effect for your team and organisation.

Three Core Elements to Self-Compassion (and Why It Matters)

There are three core elements[49] to self-compassion:

1. Self-kindness
2. Common humanity
3. Mindfulness

Together these three elements–self-kindness, common humanity and mindfulness–can help build your capacity to navigate challenges and

---

48   'Wellness at work: The promise and pitfalls'. *McKinsey Quarterly*. 26 October 2017. Accessed at https://www.mckinsey.com/business-functions/people-and-organizational-performance/our-insights/wellness-at-work-the-promise-and-pitfalls.

49   Neff, Kristin D., Rude, Stephanie S., Kirkpatrick, Kristin L. 'An examination of self-compassion in relation to positive psychological functioning and personality traits'. *Journal of Research in Personality*. 2 October 2006. Accessed at https://self-compassion.org/wp-content/uploads/publications/JRPbrief.pdf.

shocks that you might face both in your life and in your work. In other words, they allow you to build resilience as a leader.

Resilient Leadership

Resilience building is a highly promoted construct in leadership for overcoming setbacks, sustaining energy under pressure and ultimately meeting adversity. Research shows that leaders who are able to ultimately impact productivity and sustainability for the better need a safe environment where they can thrive both as individuals and organisational leaders and develop their own internal resilience (just like their teams)[50].

And resilient leadership has an incredible number of benefits:

- Resilient leaders can sustain their energy levels under pressure
- Resilient leaders cope with and adapt to disruptive changes
- Resilient leaders bounce back from setbacks
- Resilient leaders can overcome major challenges without treating themselves or others badly

In fact, resilient leadership is a critical element of high-performing leaders.[51] As a leader, you must cultivate resilience within yourself in order to thrive and succeed. And you must strive to instil it in your team as well.

---

50   Ledesma, J. 'Conceptual Frameworks and Research Models on Resilience in Leadership'. SAGE Open. 12 August 2014. Accessed at https://doi.org/10.1177/2158244014545464.

51   Kohlrieser, George, Orlick, Anouk Lavoie, Perrinjaquet, Michelle. 'Resilient leadership: Navigating the pressures of modern working life'. IMD. 28 November 2014. Accessed at https://www.imd.org/research-knowledge/articles/resilient-leadership-navigating-the-pressures-of-modern-working-life/#:~:text=Resilient%20leaders%20have%20the%20ability,dysfunctional%20behavior%20or%20harming%20others.

Putting Self-Compassion into Practice

Self-compassion seems easy enough, but it can be hard to put into practice (for example, you wouldn't say the things to a friend or an employee that you might say to yourself). But if you are committed to building self-compassion into your leadership style your team and business will certainly benefit. And the best place to start is through compassion to others.

As a leader you can mirror and build your own self-compassion, and, ultimately, more emotional intelligence, resilience and growth mindset, through compassion towards your team. Which makes your own self-compassion an unexpected benefit to add to the long list of benefits that compassion brings already. Best of all, your self-compassion (and all the benefits it brings to you) helps to make you an exceptional leader.

How to Practice Self-Compassion:

1. **Practice forgiveness.** Everyone makes mistakes. Even leaders.
2. **Embrace a growth mindset.** This is at the heart of wellbeing.
3. **Express gratitude.** It puts the focus on the good.
4. **Be generous.** This includes both thoughts and actions.
5. **Be mindful.** Watch how you speak to (and think about) yourself and others.

Self-Compassion and Becoming an Exceptional Leader

How can self-compassion make for an exceptional leader? It's because it helps to build positive psychological traits such as the ability to be less critical of yourself and being able to move through challenging circumstances. It also helps you to be more adaptable, so you are less likely to shy away from challenges and have higher confidence in yourself for success. It gives you the space to take on more responsibility and accountability[52], an element of truly exceptional leadership. And, finally, when you are more self-compassionate you are more likely to be able to encourage similar benefits in your team, peers and as an organisation as a whole— leading engaged healthy teams that reap rewards.

Coping with Compassion Fatigue

What happens when compassion fatigue does hit? While much of what we know about compassion fatigue comes from the healthcare setting and those in caregiving roles[53], but it's prevalent today in many industries, including leadership. So, courageous leaders learn how to cope with it when it does appear.

To understand how we cope with a particular response to an event, it's important to understand 'surge capacity depletion', particularly as viewed with a leadership lens. Surge capacity depletion is essentially the point at which you have used up your capacity to respond to an event, and you haven't yet had time to recover. Similar to an overwhelmed health care setting, leaders are also prone to this phenomenon when they don't actively work to restore their own tank or at least hold back some reserves.

When we are depleted as leaders, compassion, both for ourselves and for others, may be one of the first things to go, as our natural tendency under stress is to believe our own biases and see things from only our

52   Kristin D. NeV a,, Stephanie S. Rude a, Kristin L. Kirkpatrick b, An examination of self-compassion in relation to positive psychological functioning and personality traits https://self-compassion.org/wp-content/uploads/publications/JRPbrief.pdf

53   Slatten, Lisa Anne, Carson, Kerry David, Carson, Paula Phillips.' Compassion fatigue and burnout: what managers should know'. *Health Care Management*. 2011. Accessed at https://pubmed.ncbi.nlm.nih.gov/22042140/.

own perspectives. These blinkers create a situation where you're missing out on all the benefits that leading with compassion has brought to you, your team and even your organisation.

So how do we refuel, top up the tank or restore our depleted compassion? By making proactive, and consistent steps toward good mental health– also known as 'active recovery'. Implementing daily mental health habits, practising good sleep hygiene, and actively pursuing mindfulness are a few of the things I've found personally to assist in my practice. Getting in charge of your own routine and maintaining healthy boundaries can help protect your reserves of compassion.

Here are some things you might try:

- Hobbies - find something completely unrelated to your leadership career, it may be a creative endeavour or just getting out in your garden.
- Gratitude - there are many gratitude exercises out there and can be as simple as jotting down three things you are grateful for before you sit down to your daily to-do-list.
- Mindfulness - whatever that looks like for you. It could be a guided meditation before bed or writing a 'morning pages' freehand as soon as you open your eyes in the morning.
- Exercise - group fitness, walking the dog, or just dancing in your kitchen.
- Time Alone - a solitary walk or sitting for a quiet coffee in the morning.
- Time away from devices - put down the phone, take off your notifications or work emails, schedule time out for you.
- Time in Nature - get into the sunlight if you can, forest walks or even a walk around the block.

- Time with friends - be social with friends you feel supported by.
- Time out - schedule in holidays and respite. Treat this as important as you would a leadership project you are working on.

These things aren't difficult to do, and they don't require a big commitment or investment. They are also healthy habits to promote even if you aren't suffering compassion fatigue. They will still help you to cultivate healthy self-compassion making you better equipped to promote leading with compassion in your team and business.

'We all have empathy; we may not have enough courage to display it.

—Maya Angelou

Flexing Your Compassion Muscle

What does compassion look like? If we look to our early days of learning compassion we realise that it all comes back to our intrinsic understanding of what it is to be human. This is a gentle construct that often may require a sidestep from an emotional position, particularly when dealing with a tough situation or an upset team member, which can be complex. Luckily, when implementing compassion in a leadership role you are at 'the action' stage of a response and not an emotional stage (like you would be with 'empathy'). And this means you're in an excellent position to help your team members find a good solution to the challenge.

It's important to remember that compassion is not always about a solution. Sometimes it's simply about building a space of trust and psychological safety. It's concern, kindness and thoughtfulness. It involves a genuine understanding, and concern for, what the person is going through (without necessarily embodying the feeling). And while it does include having the capacity and motivation to act as a support—that doesn't always mean finding a solution to the problem. In some cases, it might just be listening.

Fostering compassion in yourself may be a case of switching yourself on to a compassionate mindset and practice and reminding yourself of the three core elements of compassion self-kindness, common humanity, and mindfulness[54]

---

54 Self-Compassion: The Proven Power of Being Kind to Yourself, Dr. Kristin Neff, https://www.amazon.com/Self-Compassion-Proven-Power-Being-Yourself/dp/0061733520

A compassionate leader will always work to keep in mind that your team members are also human and susceptible to the same negative thought patterns and self-compassion that you are. Your intention must be to continually strive to recognise different perspectives, empathise with those perspectives and exercise kindness and compassion, while keeping a handle on your own negative self-talk.

Research[55] shows that writing a letter to yourself can help. Dedicate five minutes to write a letter about the current challenges in your leadership role. Put on your compassionate lens and ask yourself what you would say to a colleague going through the same challenges? How might you encourage them? What might they observe from an objective perspective? Try to be as honest and open as you can and look at your current challenges with fresh eyes.

---

55 Breines, Juliana G., Chen, Serena. 'Self-Compassion Increases Self-Improvement Motivation'. Personality and Social Psychology Bulletin. 29 May 2012. Accessed at https://journals.sagepub.com/doi/abs/10.1177/0146167212445599.

Chapter 8

Lead With Influence

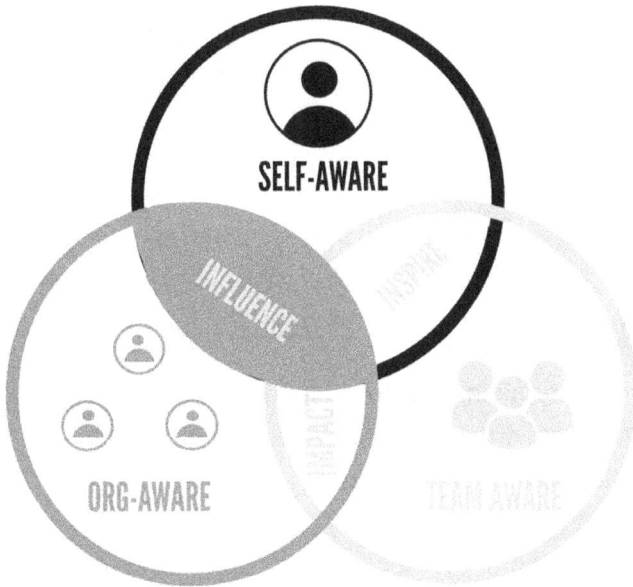

Made for More definition: Leading with influence is the ability to lead others regardless of the power that you have over their role. Drive organisation direction and adapt to changing environments.

'The key to successful leadership is influence, not authority.'

—Kenneth Blanchard

The ability to influence others is an essential leadership skill. When you can influence others, you are able to have an impact on their thoughts, ideas and opinions, and also, importantly, on their actions and decisions. Ultimately, this influence allows you to get things done and achieve desired outcomes.

At a basic level, influence is about compliance—getting someone to do something that you want them to do. But achieving genuine commitment from other people, not just base level compliance, is needed if you want to reach your goals within your team and organisation.

Rather than prescribing a course of action and having followers carry out tasks, exceptional leadership involves a collaborative effort. Yes, there must be buy-in–but it's more than giving commands. In fact, it's the art of motivating–or influencing–your team towards a common goal. In order to achieve this, exceptional and influential leaders must bring to the table an ability to strategise, energise, motivate, muster and most of all, influence.

In other words, influential leadership is an active relationship with your team that goes beyond compliance and can lead to rich, meaningful relationships with profitable and measurable outcomes.

Thinking of influence in terms of being a Courageous Leader™ means being able to have the influence to make changes and create real impact, but also have the ability to influence something or someone in a significant, and positive way. When we stay close to this meaning, we will find influential leading intuitive and really quite a simple concept.

Becoming an Influential Leader

Understanding that influence is important may seem obvious— you want other people to think or act as you do in order to achieve common goals. But really becoming an influential leader is much more than getting people to do what you want. In order to lead in a way that makes a lasting impact, you must *influence* rather than *compel*. And that means showing them the value in what you want them to do, either by your words, actions or through modelling behaviours.

The most influential leaders–those who are best at influencing others– are skilled at tapping into the motivations, emotions and underlying drivers that lead to their team's actions. You can see these influential leaders easily from the outside because they're the ones with an army of followers acting in support of their mission or cause. Look around you– now that you understand what to look for, you'll see these influential people all around the world–leaders such as Michelle Obama, Xi Jinping, Jacinda Ardern and Bob Iger. Each of these leaders has an exceptional team of people behind them, as well as the unflagging support of a core group within their community, whose actions show that they are aligned with that leader's purpose. Even better, they work to support that leader to fulfil that purpose.

Michelle Obama's Instagram account, for example, is estimated to grow by over 15,000 followers per day[55]. In fact, her profile has an average 1.30% influence rate which means each of her posts can have an

---

55   https://www.speakrj.com/audit/report/michelleobama/instagram

estimated average of 670.4K influence. And on Twitter, it's estimated that each of her tweets will reach (or influence) 15,000 people[56].

Michelle Obama has this reach because she has tapped into the emotions and motivations that drive people. She is able to engage and relate to them on that level, and then influence them to her way of thinking because they can see that she gets it, and them. In this way, she leads with influence.

Leading to Influence and Leading to Inspire–Why You Need BOTH

In Part 1 we looked at some great leaders who led by inspiration. Though there is some crossover, there is a difference between leading with influence and leading with inspiration. And this really comes down to a feeling.

- Influence means affecting or changing the way someone, or something develops, behaves or thinks.
- Inspiration is making someone *feel* that they want to do something and can do it.

This is an intangible element, but it's that intangible element that is a vital part of being able to influence others. And its why inspiration is an important aspect to tackle first in order to, ultimately, lead with influence.

There's a quote by Maya Angelou that sums this up well: Maya Angelou: 'I've learned that people will forget what you said, people will forget what you did, but people will never forget how you made them feel'.

---

56   https://www.speakrj.com/audit/report/MichelleObama/twitter

If you ensure that you have inspired your team, that you have created that feeling of wanting to do something (your goals) or follow someone (you), then you are well on your way to being able to affect or change the way they think, behave or act. You're well on your way to leading with influence.

Influence is built upon a foundation of trust

A leader who is not trusted has a limited ability to create and use influence.

So, it's important to focus on *doing* right, rather than *being* right.

When you don't just talk the talk but walk the walk, then you build trust. People will rarely make a leap of faith for someone who hasn't earned their trust.

Influence is built upon making others successful

This principle is also referred to as the law of reciprocity, or service leadership. And back in my corporate days, this was my go-to strategy for influence. I loved to raise people up, help them to become super skilled so they could accelerate their career.

Having a super-skilled team not only helped me out as the leader, but it also raised the trust within my team. As they became more successful, they had more opportunities, it helped build the reputation that I was a leader who creates other leaders.

Influence is effective if you're likeable

People do business with people they know, like and trust. It's that simple.

If you want to influence people then you need to be approachable, positive, affable and trustworthy. You have to be a person of character and integrity.

No one wants to work with someone who is standoffish, pessimistic, and untrustworthy.

Of course, as human beings, there will be times when we feel empty, grumpy or tired. When you're in this spot, have a think about how you can get back your likeability. If you need to take some time out, do it.

Self-care for leaders is important. You can't show up for your people and drive your business or team if you're not looking after yourself.

Influence is routed through helping others maintain commitments

In the leadership world, people often judge you by your ability to keep your word and deliver on your promises.

The key behind influencing via commitment lies in your ability to have people adopt an initial position that is consistent with a behaviour such that they are willing to agree to requests that are consistent with the prior commitment.

People desire to be perceived as dependable, reliable and successful and will normally go to great lengths not to have their track record or their reputation tarnished.

Gaining strong commitments early on and then simply holding people to their commitments ultimately helps them enhance their reputation for delivering on promises made.

This is a two-pronged approach. As a role model, you keep your own commitments. As a leader of people, you enable your teams to keep their word and their commitment.

So, if there's something you need to sign off on, approve or get out of the way for them, make sure you do that. This way, your people keep their commitments, and you don't create blockers along the way.

Influence is most often possessed by those with authority

As a leader, you have a huge responsibility to make sure you lead in a way that is congruent with you, and with the people around you and in alignment with the direction of the business.

It's also important to realise there is a reason for this statement, 'The highest authority is that which is given and rarely that which is taken'.

Authority is most often given to those who display honesty, competency, expertise and wisdom. With authority comes credibility and with credibility comes influence.

> 'The highest authority is that which is given and rarely that which is taken'.

Since those with the most authority will always have the most influence, it's important to remember to use your influence for the good of your people and your business. Without the ability to influence others, you will find it hard to achieve traction for your people and business.

People now recognise the importance of influence leadership. In the past, people could get away with being the "boss" and forcing people to follow top-down directions. In this new era of leadership, people don't necessarily have to listen or agree with you even if you're the leader.

Two Types of Influence in Leadership

Leadership as we know today stems from two ideologies –transactional influence and transformational influence.

Transactional Influence

Transactional leadership is based on transactional influence. It was first conceptualised by sociologist Max Weber, who stated that 'influence stems from formal hierarchical authority and defined processes—step-by-step strategy cascades, performance metrics, accountability, and the like.'

This method is most similar to an authoritative view when it comes to leadership and is generally seen in a business that really embraces hierarchy (for example, a bank). It presents as more rigid and goals oriented, and leadership within this method operates via a fairly strict chain of command. his means that people at the top of the company, like CEOs or senior management, make key decisions that are acted upon by the rest of the organisation. In some ways you can think of it like a sports team. While there is certainly motivation to succeed, success within the strict rules and demands of the game, as well as the requirements of the coaches and other players.

Although it can certainly get results, particularly against other organisations that adopt the same methodology[57], transactional leadership doesn't breed the elite leadership skills or create courageous leaders. Those who embrace or follow transactional leadership may

---

57   What is Transactional Leadership? How Structure Leads to Results. https://online.stu.edu/articles/education/what-is-transactional-leadership.aspx

struggle to build a growth mindset, encourage curious conversations, develop emotional intelligence or cultivate compassion in themselves, their team, or at an organisation level.

There are times when transactional influence is vital for the success of a business, however. For example, this approach is highly successful in a crisis, as well as with projects that require linear and specific processes. In that way, it's necessary to have this methodology up your sleeve to be able to take control in those situations.

Transformational Influence

Now let's compare transactional influence with transformational influence. While leaders who lead with transactional influence follow a strict hierarchy, leaders who follow the transformational influence approach get things done by encouragement, support and going above and beyond the call of duty.

Transformational influence is rooted in empathy and is typically utilised in workplaces with a flat structure. Unlike hierarchical organisations, where leadership, ideas and power come from the top down, transformational organisations use influence to motivate, encourage, uplift and inspire those that they lead.

In this collaborative approach, leaders and teams work together to establish desired changes and outcomes and this often drives the desire to go above and beyond the more basic requirements necessary to get the job done. Since this type of leadership often occurs in flat structures, in practice there are fewer actual leaders. But the leaders that are operating have a vested interest in both business success and the individual success for each member of the team. In return this encourages loyalty, reduces turnover and, because they share a motivating passion, the members of the team are engaged and motivated to realise their collective vision.

Research[58] from psychologist and leadership expert Ronald E. Riggio demonstrates that groups led by transformational leaders have exceptionally high levels of performance and satisfaction, more so than groups led by any other type of leaders.

Influencing Those Around You

Effective leaders don't just command. They inspire, motivate and encourage. They tap into the knowledge and skills of a group, they encourage and lead towards common goals, they inspire commitment, and they achieve exceptional results.

This is widely acknowledged to be a better way to lead, with even the US military making adjustments towards this method. In fact, in an interview with *Forbes* American general Stanley McChrystal related what he told his troops, 'If and when we get on the ground the order, we gave you is wrong, execute the order we should've given you'[59].

But how do they do that?

By cultivating the essential human skills that lead to influence.

---

58 Riggio, Ronald. 'Are You a Transformational Leader?' Psychology Today. 24 March 2009. Accessed at https://www.psychologytoday.com/au/blog/cutting-edge-leadership/200903/are-you-transformational-leader.

59 Karlgaard, Rich. 'Combat Consultant Q&A With Retired General Stanley McChrystal.' *Forbes*. 3 October 2017. Accessed at https://www.forbes.com/sites/richkarlgaard/2017/10/03/combat-consultant-qa-with-retired-general-stanley-mc-chrystal/?sh=1e64ee0b2f44.

5 Human Traits of Influential Leaders

Influential leadership helps you to lead with humanity. And that means you can fall back on, rely on and utilise many of the basic human traits that you already foster. While we want to make an impact, a lasting impression in an important way, on our teams and in our wider organisation, to do that we simply need to amplify these human traits in our leadership, and foster an environment built on these core values.

1. **Trustworthy:** when we are a trusted person in an organisation you become a person of influence; when you earn the trust of your peers, colleagues, and team you become a safe choice. Ultimately you will foster more buy-in when it comes to having influence and reaching for success.

2. **Reciprocity:** although this sounds more transactional in principle, we need to remember that influence is a two-way street. If you, as a leader, understand that you have to invest in your team to empower their success they will be more likely to have a vested interest in return.

3. **Relatability:** when you are open, positive, likeable and accessible you will find it easier to connect on a genuine level and create more relationships and, because of that, influence.

4. **Reliability:** as well as being relatable you must also be reliable in doing what you say. This builds trust and commitment and demonstrates that you can 'walk the walk'.

5. **Credibility:** known as a prerequisite for influence, credibility is having authority and being known to have power. This demonstrates that you are a reliable choice to influence others.

Developing Your Human Traits

You may already have these, and more, traits. But if you are a leader looking to raise your profile as a leader with influence there are some ways to showcase your skills to advance your own leadership goals and have a domino effect on organisational success.

- **Raise your profile:** build a reputation on what you want to be known for and be intentional with what your unique influence is and how you present it to the world. Become your own personal brand showcasing what distinguishes you as a leader.

- **Become the obvious choice:** chase the opportunities that allow you to demonstrate your reputation for competence and reliability. Proactively seek opportunities to display your ability to lead the way with creative solutions

- **Build a network:** creating leverage amongst your networks to position yourself as a valuable choice when it comes to utilising your wide networks that will be a benefit to yourself and the team as a whole. It's more than networking–its building valuable connections that benefit all involved.

- **Connection:** create genuine connections at every opportunity. Let go of transactional relationships and focus on spending time on and showing interest in the real people behind the role to forge rich and authentic connections.

- **Always be the influencer:** role model influential leadership traits from day one even if you are not yet placed in your 'dream' leadership role. Modelling your leadership personality traits won't go unnoticed.

How To Successfully Lead and Communicate With Influence

It's a misconception that when you finally land that dream role or title, you will instantly obtain the respect and admiration that you need as an influential leader. It's true a job title may make you eligible to manage your staff, but leading people is an entirely different game. Leading with influence is about building transformation and, of course, results.

As we've learned previously, displaying leadership traits can help in this process. Here are some lessons to remind yourself when you find leading with influence on the challenging side of things:

Leave defensiveness at the door.

As we learned in curious conversations, instilling curiosity in your practice as a leader can encourage open conversations and inspire more creative problem solving. Actively choose to leave defensiveness at the door. If someone raises a concern or issue, it's an opportunity for you to display your courageous leadership and not take it personally. Use this as a moment to change a negative into a positive.

Put on your curious and compassionate lens.

When you come across challenges in leadership, rely on your elite human traits that we can carry you through. Remaining human will always keep you in good stead. Engage in self-compassion as you would for an employee or a colleague. Ask open-ended questions with the true intent to learn. Your ability to remain objective and positive as a leader through challenging times will benefit your team.

Engage your own emotional intelligence.

Be aware of your own emotions–you've worked hard to get where you are today, and you are entitled to feel the emotional charge that comes along with the peaks and troughs of leadership. Incorporating daily healthy habits can help you keep your emotions on track and remain self-aware.

Practise gratitude.

Give recognition to yourself and to others. Remember the important leadership trait of influential leaders, reciprocity? Think about ways you can demonstrate your gratitude to your team today, not for anything in return, but as a genuine way of showing who you are–an authentic, grateful leader.

Be compassionate.

Flexing your compassion muscle can help you be a positive influence and a trusted person by providing a psychologically safe space for support. Also using compassion can redirect an emotional response to a place of action and solution.

Empower.

Lead by example. Show that you are in charge of your own interpretation of an event, feeling or situation. Role model making the positive choice even when things get tough. Making the most of a difficult time, learning from an experience and choosing a positive demeanour can filter down to the team as a whole.

Choose happiness.

Happiness is a choice[60]. When you're presented with information or a situation, you have a choice of how you will respond and how you will feel. You can choose to interpret the information in a way that makes you feel great! And you can choose to do the opposite. You are the only one that can determine the state of your own emotions. Choose happiness. When you do, you can positively influence those around you, raising energy levels and driving engagement and commitment.

The Perks of being an Influential Leader

Of course, leading with influence is not all about the challenges. It also brings some important positive impacts on your own personal development and your business as a whole.

At heart, you are working to become an exceptional leader who is able to facilitate change, bring out the best in people and, ultimately, make an impact in your organisation and even within your chosen field. Influential leadership can give that to you. You are also able to reach greater personal satisfaction, increased job satisfaction and the opportunity to create mutual success among your team—all causes for celebration and desirable perks. Finally, when you utilise the influential leadership techniques, you'll be instrumental in retaining an engaged and connected workforce and motivating and inspiring your team.

By displaying these highly desirable human traits to create rich and meaningful relationships, you can develop your influence more than you might imagine. Furthermore, by implementing some of the more

---

60   Yuna L. Ferguson & Kennon M. Sheldon (2013) Trying to be happier really can work: Two experimental studies, The Journal of Positive Psychology, 8:1, 23-33, DOI: 10.1080/17439760.2012.747000, https://www.tandfonline.com/doi/abs/10.108 0/17439760.2012.747000, accessed 29 October 2021.

practicable tips you will exercise your influence and be able to actively gauge your success.

Ultimately, when you embrace the influential leadership style you'll also up the ante in 'relationship capital'. This is a subtle, but powerful advantage to any leader, or potential leader, as you develop excellent relationships that start small and intensify with time. This capital isn't necessarily something that can be learned but built upon through time, thoughtfulness, reliability and trust.

Flexing Your Influence Muscle

Building influence in the workplace takes time and energy, but it can have a long-lasting ripple effect. Through it you can shape your organisation's culture, commitment, engagement, decisions and even strategic direction.

As you build your influence, you will be making an impact on others. And you'll be making an impact on yourself as well. Look for these moments—see where you're modelling behaviours that exceptional leaders have. Keep your eyes open for the developing trust from others, and the feedback and response you're getting. Watch out for the celebrations of mutual success. Review how you and your team have managed through challenges. And look to see what meaningful relationships you have, and are, developing.

These are the moments that show you what it means to influence people, so you can do more of just that in the future.

Part 3

Organisation-Aware (Lead Your Organisation)

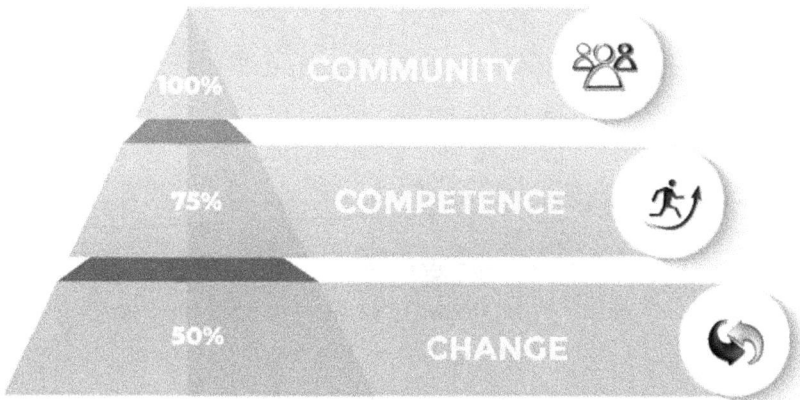

Made For More definition: To achieve our objectives and effectively navigate the future, we need to create leaders who are strategic across all areas of business.

"Basically, to lead without a title
is to derive your power within
the organisation not from your
position but from your competence,
effectiveness, relationship,
excellence, innovation and ethics."

—Robin Sharma

So far, we've discussed leading ourselves and leading our team. Now we want to tackle how to lead within an organisation. Because to achieve our objectives and effectively navigate the future, we need to create leaders who are strategic across all areas of business.

If you look at the top strategic leaders of our time, they're all focused on the same things – strategy, development, communication and community. But to be a strong leader for the overall business, they apply these categories to the organisation as a whole.

You'll recognise these leaders for their intuitive leaps, they're strong leadership through crises, and their ability to recognise patterns and push for new insights. As Finland's former president, J.K. Paasikivi said[61], 'wisdom begins by recognising the facts and then re-recognising

---

61 Schoemaker, Paul J.H., Krupp, Steve, Howland, Samatha. 'Strategic Leadership: The Essential Skills'. Harvard Business Review. January–February 2013. Accessed at https://hbr.org/2013/01/strategic-leadership-the-esssential-skills.

or rethinking them to expose their hidden implications'. That's what a strategic leader does.

The Key Elements of a Strategic Organisational Leader

A strategic organisational leader is focused on three key elements:

- Change Leadership (Organisational Strategy) - The capability to step outside of your comfort zone to meet the challenges that lie ahead. For the purpose of developing resilience and the ability to bounce back
- Competence (Organisational Development) – The desire and commitment to do something successful or efficiently individually, as a team or organisationally, for the purposed of excellent rather than mediocre.
- Community (Organisational Culture) – Building a network of people who can be relied upon and referred to in times of collaboration and/or crisis. Developing a send of belonging within a team and organisation.

Chapter 9

Change Leadership

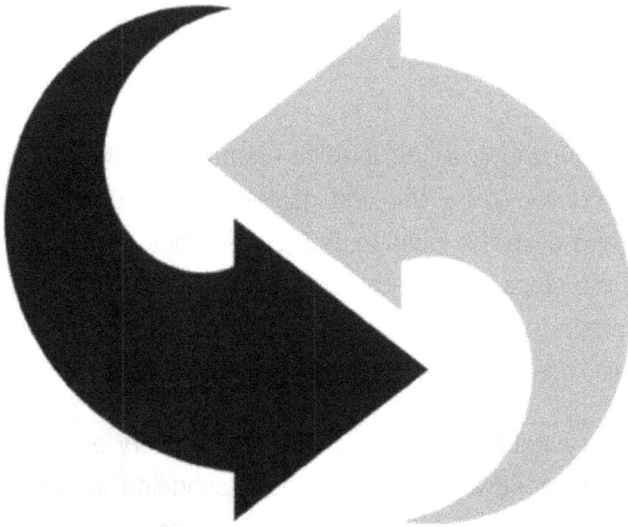

Made For More Definition: The capability to step outside your comfort zone to meet the challenges that lie ahead, for the purpose of developing resilience and the ability to bounce back.

> "Leaders are the ones who have the courage to go first, to put themselves at personal risk to open a path for others to follow."
>
> —Simon Sinek

Change leadership is a little bit like creating a ballet. You know the concept and you know the end goal—the performance. You know the date and even the location. But it's developing the choreography, teaching the steps, casting the dancers and designing the costumes and the props that's the messy bit in the middle. This is change. And you can also see how it is also organisational strategy.

Change is inevitable in every industry and in every organisation. And organisations worldwide have seen how technological advancements and a global pandemic have significantly increased the rate at which change happens.

As John F. Kennedy famously said, 'Change is the law of life, and those who look on to the past or present are certain to miss the future.'

In 2019 I was at a conference where futurist Stephan Yarwood was one of the speakers. During his talk he spoke about the rapid pace of change happening in the world at the moment. He said that it was getting harder and harder to imagine what's coming next— the conceptual ideas.

Yarwood went on to share an example of artificial Intelligence that could occur in everyday life. Imagine walking down the street with your Fitbit or smart watch, and you get a notification that you're a five-minute walk away from your next destination.

Your heart rate is slightly elevated, and your body temperature is also slightly elevated because of the exercise, so the next notification you receive suggests that you move to your left by one metre on the footpath. Turns out your wearable AI has just synced up with the Wi-Fi in the nearby lamppost and is indicating to you that there's a breeze that will cool you down. It knows you have a meeting shortly and is suggesting this change before you start perspiring and become an unprofessional sweaty mess.

Crazy huh?

There is so much that we don't know about what is coming. As a leader, being able to rapidly adapt and flex is key to remaining relevant and resilient in this day and age and an increasingly important aspect of a successful business. As a result, a range of tools and techniques have been devised to aid businesses during change. However, for changes to be properly embedded within an organisation, minimising disruption and becoming part of business as usual, change management tools and skills are not enough.

> Being able to rapidly adapt and flex is key to remaining relevant and resilient in this day and age.

Change leadership is key.

Managing and leading through change is a core business activity. Great organisational leaders must be prepared to innovate and implement solutions when the organisation is faced with unexpected change or crises. They need to view this as an opportunity and develop the skills to be ready to lead the team in a new direction. But too often we focus on the *management* side of change, rather than the *leadership* side. And that's where things go wrong.

What is Change Management?

Change management is simply a term that refers to all the ways in which organisations prepare, support and lead their staff and teams when facing organisational change. Many leaders see this as a linear process. So, one that has a set end goal and predetermined checkpoints or milestones. These milestones are set by managers and implemented by team members that they believe are the best suited to take that particular action.

The entire process tends to have a discrete beginning and end, with distinct 'projects' contained within it. It often addresses only one or two big-ticket items (for example, implementing a new IT system) and the remaining ancillary areas of the organisation that aren't captured within those projects, are left to languish, or fall behind.

As anyone who has been through a major change in an organisation knows, it is rarely a straightforward process. It involves trial and error and an understanding of the organisational strategy as a whole and where each area intersects with the others so that the process can envelop all the operational elements of the business. This requires strong leadership, input from throughout the organisation and course-corrections along the way. So, to bring the biggest benefit, implementing change requires more than just management—it requires change leadership.

What is Change Leadership?

When Alan Mulally was appointed Ford President and CEO in 2006, he began what would become decisive and significant changes for the Ford company, called 'The Way Forward" restructuring plan. This introduced a central idea—'One Ford'—which had the company focussing on its core brands.

They sold off Jaguar, Land Rover, Aston Martin and Volvo, and then borrowed $23.6 billion dollars as a cushion and stabilisation fund, which was crucial for getting the company through the subsequent global financial crisis. The One Ford plan also introduced massive cost-cutting (including suspension of dividends to shareholders) and downsizing their workforce by 43%.

As you can imagine, this raft of changes could have been disastrous for company culture. But Alan Mulally knew that. And he implemented substantial changes that would promote greater transparency and accountability, such as Thursday, 7am meetings with his deputies where they talked about operations and issues. He moved his office from the top floor to the fourth, where the engineers were based, so he could be there for face-to-face communication and engagement.

Mulally also responded to employee emails by attending their offices in person or calling them. He sold the company jets and limited perks for the top execs, including himself. And he demonstrated an unwavering commitment to these changes.

The result? The change proposals met with minimum resistance across the board, even though a huge proportion of the Ford workforce was negatively affected. Mulally's ability to lead through change (rather than manage change) was the driver for getting employees behind and supporting his vision.

Change Leaders Inspire a Vision

As you can see from the Ford example, change leadership is a proactive approach to change management. Whenever an organisation has a task to accomplish, they need this goal to be clearly defined and they need a vision for how they (and their teams) will achieve that goal. When it comes to leading through change, this vision is equally important.

In fact, change should be understood to be an opportunity for growth and improvement rather than a finite project. Change leaders must lead with a vision – a vision that can inspire individuals as well as the collective in the form of teams. And they must be able to advocate for that vision throughout the entire organisation.

Change Leaders Take a People First Approach

In order to successfully lead through change, leaders must take a people-first approach. Every decision they make and action they take must first consider the impact on their people, including how any change affects employees, their processes and their tools. Successful change leaders work collaboratively alongside company leaders, the human resources team and employees with a goal to integrate the change strategically and even thoughtfully rather than just impose it forcefully.

Before any change initiative is started, change leaders must do the work to build trust with their employees. This creates the relationships that will provide a strong foundation for employees even when things are in chaos or upheaval. It allows them to follow and support the change plan despite any uncertainties.

As part of a people-centric approach, change leaders value the insights and feedback they get from their team. They communicate with them directly and often to try to understand the challenges that the change might be causing individually, within the team structure or even within the organisation as a whole. This gives employees a voice in the change strategy – and the actions and decisions that are being made in support of that strategy – empowering them to provide the input to feel engaged with the process every step of the way...

Most importantly, a change leader (as opposed to simply a change manager) has the courage to acknowledge when things aren't working as anticipated. And they have a flexible mindset that allows them to adjust the plan accordingly to take into account this new information and changes.

Why is (Organisational) Change So Hard?

All change is hard – organisational change being just one type. As human beings, we are conditioned to prefer stability. In fact, research[62] shows that all measures of stress – whether that's subjective or objective – were at their absolute highest when predictability is low (in this case it was 50%).

When our routine, or predictable patterns, are upset due to change, we're left with a high level of anxiety and fear. This happens even when we are the ones who are choosing to implement the change in our lives. But it's also notoriously hard, and perhaps even harder, when we're having to deal with organisational change.

Here's why:

1. **Organisational change is not self-directed.** By its very nature, organisational change is born out of external pressure—from economic change, shareholders, customers or competitors. Because of this, we lose our own autonomy

---

62 de Berker, A., Rutledge, R., Mathys, C. et al. 'Computations of uncertainty mediate acute stress responses in humans'. Nature Communications. 7, 10996 (2016). https://doi.org/10.1038/ncomms10996.

and feelings of control. The sense that we are in charge of our own lives is gone, and that is a feeling that is difficult for more humans to accept.

2. **Organisational change can be overwhelming and confusing.** Too often changes are decided on and acted upon in 'secret' – or what feels like secret to those who aren't privy to them. While the decision makers then have the benefit of time to come to terms with the expected disruptions, and prepare for them, the receivers of change (the employees) don't have that opportunity. They can often feel that changes are being thrust upon them, with very little warning and often huge information gaps. It leaves them feeling overwhelmed and confused.

3. **Organisational change can mean uncertainties about job security.** Transformation is often the engine used to drive efficiencies, and that can lead to a lot of uncertainties in terms of job security. And it's a justified fear, because just as with Ford, sometimes this does mean downsizing the workforce.

When change does lead to employee restructuring, and it's not handled well, motivation is lost. People no longer strive to improve or be the best or even to continue performing at a high standard. Instead, they start to focus on simply surviving.

The Three Cs of Change Leadership

Change necessarily includes two parts – the process and the people. As change leaders, we need to have the skills to connect these two pieces of the puzzle in order to create effective change leadership. In fact, when they are brought together, they can help manage some of those difficulties we explored above. Those skills can be thought of as the three Cs of effective change leadership[63]:

Communicate

Unsuccessful leaders tend to focus on the 'what' behind the change (i.e., what is changing on a granular level). But successful change leaders don't just focus on the 'what' – they also communicate the 'why.'

This is a vital part of change leadership because it's the 'why', the purpose behind the change, that creates the strongest buy-in and engagement from employees. And this is strengthened further when it's connected to the organisation's predetermined values.

Collaborate

Another critical part of change leadership is the ability to collaborate. Successful leaders work across boundaries, bringing people together to plan and execute change, encouraging them to break out of their silos and promoting healthy communication.

The best change leaders also include their employees in decision-making early on, which strengthens their openness and commitment to change.

Commit

Successful leaders also model the beliefs and behaviours they want to see in their employees. They demonstrate their own commitment by devoting time to the change effort. They adapt to challenges, convey

---

63   Hole, Glenn. 'The 3 C's of Change Leadership'. 28 May 2020. Accessed at https://www.dr-glennhole.org/the-3-cs-of-change-leadership/#:~:text=The%203%20C's%20unite%20effective,Communicate.&text=Leaders%20who%20explains%20through%20communication,Collaborate.

a positive attitude, are persistent and patient and are willing to step outside of their comfort zones to reach results. When their employees see these behaviours, they tend to follow as well.

When we communicate, collaborate and commit as leaders, we're able to bring the process of change together with the people, making both works more seamlessly together as one unit. It also helps to stop employees from worrying about issues that would make the change harder – such as the risk of job loss. This makes implementing strategy change more efficient as well.

Leading the Process of Change

Strategic change doesn't happen on its own. It needs strong change leaders to effectively guide the process (as opposed to the people) from conceptualisation to implementation. So, leading the process of change takes something more – including these three key competencies:

Initiate. When it comes to leading the process of change, change leaders need to first understand the need for change. Once they understand the need themselves, then they can begin making the case for the change they seek with the rest of their teams. This is change initiation.

Effective change leaders will use evidence to demonstrate the purpose and vision for the change, and the desired outcomes, including evaluating the business context, and identifying a common goal. It's this common understanding of a goal that helps others to buy in to the process and focus on the necessary tasks to accomplish the end goal.

Strategise. Successful change leadership requires two things – a strategy and a clear action plan. The overarching strategy creates the goalposts that will drive the team forward, while the action plan lays out the priorities, timelines, tasks, structures, behaviours, and resources required to meet that strategy. In every case change management need to both identify what should change, and also what should remain the same.

Execute. Now it's time to execute, and when it comes to the process of change management, execution simply involves translating strategy into action. Of course, a simple definition doesn't necessarily mean a simple process. The execution of your change management process is one of the most important things you will do as a change leader.

To do it well, change leaders need to focus on getting key people into key positions. Sometimes, as noted above, this may mean removing some staff, or even eliminating some projects to focus on strategic wins. Another excellent method to undertake during the execution phase is the breaking down of big projects into small wins. This helps you accumulate early victories and build momentum towards your goal.

Measure. Each of these steps requires that you gather data, analyse metrics and put monitoring systems into place in order to measure progress. If you don't know where you've been, it will be difficult to understand if you're heading in the right direction.

It's important to note that as organisations evolve over time, stability and change must exist in tandem. This is a particular polarity in the process side of change management and one that needs to be properly managed in order to help your organisation achieve its full potential. As a change leader you'll need to find the sweet spot between stability and change, learning where to embrace disruption (for example, in what key roles) and where to maintain the status quo (for example, systems that can overarch both the current activities and those in the changed organisation).

Leading People Through Change

Formal change processes are often fairly well understood. But the people side of change leadership is often forgotten. In fact, the most effective leaders devote a great deal of time, resources, energy and effort to engage those people involved in or impacted by the change.

So, what techniques and strategies do effective change leaders utilise in order to lead *people* through change?

Give time to adapt. Firstly, they understand that people need time to adapt to change. This is particularly important where the change initiative is fast-moving. In those cases, some leaders might feel pressure to push on, rather than pulling back and helping their people process the change. But that is actually a mistake. Whenever possible, helping people to process these changes in an adaptive manner should be the approach taken.

Provide support. You can often recognise a successful change project because of the success of the people within it. And that's because excellent change leaders work hard to remove any barriers to employee success. Within the change environment, this can include personal barriers such as wounded egos. Or it can include professional barriers such as a lack of training to take on roles within the changed organisation.

However, successful change leaders will be focused on providing support to their people, while still working towards their goals, rather than exclusively focussing on results. This may mean providing opportunities for training or working with strong communication in order to soothe any ego issues.

Have sway. Sway is simply influence, and like influence, it's not about getting blind obedience, but about demonstrating to others the purpose and reason behind the change. Because of this they are then able to raise the commitment required to drive change.

In order to create sway, change leaders need to understand what 'buy-in' looks like from their staff and stakeholders. They will need to map out the critical change agents, identify key stakeholders and effectively and efficiently communicate their vision of successful change to them.

Be willing to learn. One key quality that distinguishes successful change leaders from the unsuccessful is that they never believe they have all the answers. In fact, they're not only willing to learn, but driven to learn, to achieve more and better all the time. They ask questions, they gather feedback, and they make adjustments to their processes and strategies during the change based on the information and feedback they receive.

Engage with smart staff. A change leader who can lead their people through transition, flexibly responding to challenges is important. But an excellent change leader is actually an excellent facilitator – one who can lead people through transition, flexibly responding to challenges, by listening and engaging with the smart staff that they built around themselves.

Richard Branson said, 'It's all about finding and hiring people smarter than you. Getting them to join your business. And giving them good work. Then getting out of their way. And trusting them. You have to get out of the way so YOU can focus on the bigger vision'.

This is precisely your job as a change leader – to be a facilitator who positions the team to succeed, then gives them the space and empowers them with the authority and autonomy to do so.

Never assume understanding. An effective change leader never assumes that another person has understood them. Instead, they spend the time necessary to engage in a two-way conversation that digs deep into the issue and demonstrates a two-way understanding.

To do this well you can talk through examples and applications of the task or issue you're dealing with. You can hear their perspective and provide your own. And you can see through any filters or mental models that might have caused them to misinterpret what you were saying or asking.

Taking the time to converse about the issue gives you the opportunity to clarify and explain so misunderstandings don't occur. But you won't have this opportunity, and you'll open yourself and your staff up to mistakes, errors and upset, if you assume that others have understood without further investigation.

Model and encourage resilience. When navigating change, resilience is required because it helps people handle change's inherent pressure, uncertainty and setbacks. But resilience isn't just something staff and employees need to cultivate – leaders need to build their own reserves as well. A big part of this is taking control of your mental and physical health and demonstrating to your team that it is important. By modelling this behaviour, you're in a stronger position to guide others to face change in healthy ways as well.

Modern workplaces are change environments. Because of this, employees today need to be flexible, adaptive and, most of all, resilient. Research[64] shows that resilient workers are 'more able to manage inevitable changes and deal with novel scenarios. They are also more skilled at dealing with setbacks and have the capacity to move on

---

64   Craig, Heather. 'Resilience in the Workplace: How to Be More Resilient at Work'. Positive Psychology. 5 February 2022. Accessed at https://positivepsychology.com/resilience-in-the-workplace/.

after they encounter a stumbling block'. These are vital characteristics for your staff – and for you as their change leader. Adopting these behaviours within yourself is the first step.

Necessary Skills For Effective Change Leadership

As we've already explored, leading the *people* and the *process* of change takes certain skill sets to do well. But these are underpinned by skills that are required to be an effective change leader across the board.

Organisations today will struggle with potential disruptors. We've seen this come into play because of financial crises, pandemics, digital disruptions, global competition and changing customer expectations. And the future will see more and more of this happening.

An organisation must be willing and able to make changes to adapt to their environment. And to do this, they must have leaders who are skilled at leading change efforts. However, many leaders who are expected to have these skills, simply aren't taught them. And they may have little to no experience in this area either.

If this is you, you are not alone. Change leadership is not often understood, and even less often taught, despite the fact that nearly 50% of employees believe that it's a top requirement for senior management[65].

Research collected over the past decade from 103,474 leaders worldwide shows that there are five vital skills that impact on a leader's ability to guide their organisation through change[66]. Developing these

---

65 Folkman, Joseph. '5 Required Skills for Leading Change'. Forbes. 16 January 2020. Accessed at https://www.forbes.com/sites/joefolkman/2020/01/16/5-re-quired-skills-for-leading-change/?sh=6bb1a2df6a16.

66 Ibid.

skills within yourself will take you a long way to becoming an excellent change leader.

1. Foster Innovation

The research shows that one of the most important ingredients for an excellent change leader was innovation[67]. Too often leaders push forward, looking towards their final result or outcome, without taking the time to consider whether there are better, more innovative or creative options that can do the job better.

The key here is that you need to create space for innovation within your team or organisation. They may have brilliant ideas brewing. But they need your support and backing in order to see that idea, and bring it to life.

2. Act Quickly

An ability to act and react quickly and flexibly are vital skills when leading change, and the research shows that those leaders who have this skill are often the best at change leadership[68].

When you drop a child off for Kindy there may be tears (at least there were in my case!). But parents are taught that it's best to say a succinct (but loving!) goodbye and leave, allowing your child the chance to move onto the next thing quickly. The long goodbye gives them more chances to feel all those feelings and to elevate from upset to full blown tantrum.

This is a simple example, but it's not too dissimilar to what occurs within an organisation if a change process has languished or even stalled. This simply increases the difficulty, pain and, therefore, resistance. While you don't want to toss your employees into the deep end. Making quick

---

67   Ibid.
68   Ibid.

decisions and taking responsive action allows them to move into the next stage without wallowing too long.

3. Maintain Strategic Perspective

The third skill the research identified is a strong and well-maintained strategic perspective. Leaders who have this skill understand the goal of the change and the direction that the organisation is aspiring to. They understand the strategy, and how implementing strategic changes will lead the organisation closer to achieving their objectives.

If you don't keep your eye on the prize (the ultimate goal), you're liable to get too caught up on the change process itself, forgetting what the change is for. That makes motivating your team and driving change activities far more difficult.

4. Develop External Perspective

The fourth skill that excellent change leaders demonstrate is a good external perspective. This means that they are able to see the big picture and understand the factors happening outside of the organisation that are impacting on the change. This might be things going on in the world generally, or even changes going on with your customer base.

Looking only internally is like putting on a set of blinders. You might be highly focused, but you'll only be receiving half the necessary information

On the other hand, keeping an external perspective means keeping your eyes wide open and helps everyone understand why the change is necessary and the value that it can bring.

5. Inspire and Motivate

The last component of exceptional change leaders is one that we've dealt with a lot in our courageous leadership conversation – and that's the ability to inspire and motivate. When it comes to change leadership, this is even more vital to a successful process. Many leaders have a habit of pushing their teams when they want to reach a goal. This isn't necessarily bad, as a bit of pushing helps everyone to continue to move forward. However, the research shows that the best leaders combine the push, that is the drive for results, with a pull, which is where we lead by inspiring and motivating[69]. This combined process leads to a much better experience for the individuals on the team, and much better outcomes for the organisation as a whole.

Many leaders' first impulse is to initiate the change process with a big push. Pushing behaviours are those that focus on deadlines, timeliness, accountability, direction, deliverables and orders. Pushing is helpful because it forces everyone to move forward, lacking no other alternative. Most change efforts naturally begin with a big push. But pushing makes change a hardship with no alternatives. When leaders combine push (driving for results) and pull (inspire and motivate) the outcome is much better.

---

69   Ibid.

Flexing Your Change Leadership Muscle

Leading through change takes a large number of skills. It requires you to understand the process of change (and lead through that). It requires you to take a people-centric approach to change (and be able to lead them through that process). And it requires you to have skills that go beyond traditional leadership capabilities – including innovation, motivation, inspiration, a strategic and external perspective and the ability to act quickly and flexibly.

But at the end of the day, if you are a leader who possesses (or develops) these skills, you can be highly effective at leading change. This means that your organisation will benefit, of course. But it also means that all those people who work with you will benefit as well because you will have the ability to lead them confidently and well through the change process.

At the end of the day, your ballet will be perfectly executed, and the performance (or the achievement of your end goal) will look easy and flawless from the outside. And only you will know the messy bit in the middle that you had to conquer to get there.

Chapter 10

Competence (Organisational Development)

Made For More Definition: Competence is the desire
and commitment to do something successfully
or efficiently for the purpose of excellence.

> "Effective leadership is the
> only competitive advantage
> that will endure. That's because
> leadership has two sides, what a
> person is – character and what a
> person does – competence."
>
> —Stephen Covey

A few years ago, I was working with a client named Neil, the CEO of an Australian organisation. He came to me because, as he described it, he kept looking to 'break something'. You see, things were actually going too well for his organisation, and it was due, in great part, to the long days, late nights, and blood sweat and tears he'd taken to turn around his organisation.

All of this hard work had created great results for the executive and broader teams as well as the organisation. But now Neil was losing sleep worrying that there was something he was missing – something that he wasn't even aware of, and all because it seemed *too easy*. Easy to the point where he was constantly looking at things to break so that he could fix them again.

The problem here is that while Neil had clearly built a high level of competence into his organisation, he didn't recognise it well enough. He wasn't truly aware at what level of competence his company actually needed versus what it had so that he could safely trust that he'd filled all the gaps and was strategising well towards the future. And that would help him sleep better at night.

When you're looking to build competency across your team and organisation, you don't have to be all the things, to all the people. But you do need to know what you don't know. It's only in this way that you know where to fill the gaps.

Let's compare it with the next story, which highlights why it's important to know what you know.

A giant ship had a massive engine failure. The ship's owners tried a number of different professionals who attempted to fix it. But none of them were able to figure out the problem or even get close to fixing the broken engine.

Eventually they found an old repairman who had been fixing ships since he was very young. He arrived with a large bag of tools and immediately set to work inspecting the engine. He looked it over carefully, from top to bottom, puzzling over the problem.

Two of the ship's owners were on the ship, watching the repairman perform his considerations. They were concerned that he might not know what to do either. But they needn't have worried. After looking things over for a few minutes, the old man reached into his bag and pulled out a single, small hammer and gently tapped something within the engine. Instantly, the engine spluttered into life. The repairman carefully put his hammer away while the owners thanked him effusively for fixing the engine.

A week later, the owners received an invoice from the repairman. It was in the amount of $10,000. They were shocked, complaining to each other that he'd hardly done anything. He'd just made one small tap!

They wrote to the repairman and asked him to send an itemised invoice, wanting to know why he thought he was justified in charging such a large sum for such a small amount of work.

The repairman sent an invoice that read:

Tapping with a hammer...................... $1.00

Knowing where to tap......................... $9,999.00

Effort is important but experience and knowing where to direct that effort makes all the difference.

I like the story because it shows how small things can have big effects; and sometimes you need a guy who knows where to knock.

> True competence isn't knowing how to hit the hammer, but knowing where to tap.

True competence mastery isn't knowing how to hit the hammer but knowing where to look.

Knowing Where to Tap

As this story shows, true competence isn't knowing how to hit the hammer, but knowing where to tap. It's understanding and trusting what you know and believing that your own skills will get you to the outcomes you need. This applies to the individual, to the team and to the organisation – all of whom can develop the competencies to know where to tap the hammer.

Directing Your Effort

The other element this story highlights is around the notion of effort and competency. Effort is important but experience and knowing where to direct that effort makes all the difference. Small things can have big effects. And small efforts can lead to big outcomes. Sometimes you just need a guy who knows where to tap. The effort has been built in through the years of experience, facing challenges and learning. So even though it may appear that the expert 'isn't doing much', it's just those years of experience coalescing into true competence.

> Effort is important but experience and knowing where to direct that effort makes all the difference.

Competency and Courageous Leadership™

'Competence goes beyond words. It's the leader's ability to say it, plan it, and do it in such a way that others know that you know how — and know they want to follow you.'

—John C. Maxwell

For a Courageous Leader™, competency has to be built individually, and then it has to be built within the team and organisation as a whole. Leadership competencies are skills and behaviours that contribute to a superior performance of the leader. But organisational competencies are those that are developed within the organisation and lead to a superior performance of that organisation.

As the Courageous Leader™, it's your job to lead your team and organisation along a development path that will help them to gain the competencies that the organisation needs. These competencies amount to the suite of behaviours, attitudes, skills, knowledge and information that elevate the performance as a whole. Of course, it's confidence in your own competency and ability that will motivate your team to follow you too.

Organisational Competencies

Organisational competencies are the core competencies that define what a company does best, and how they want to accomplish that success. Some of these competencies could be:

- Communication
- Problem-solving
- Strategic perspective
- Resilience
- Innovation
- Customer care
- Teamwork
- Agility

The Conscious Competence Model

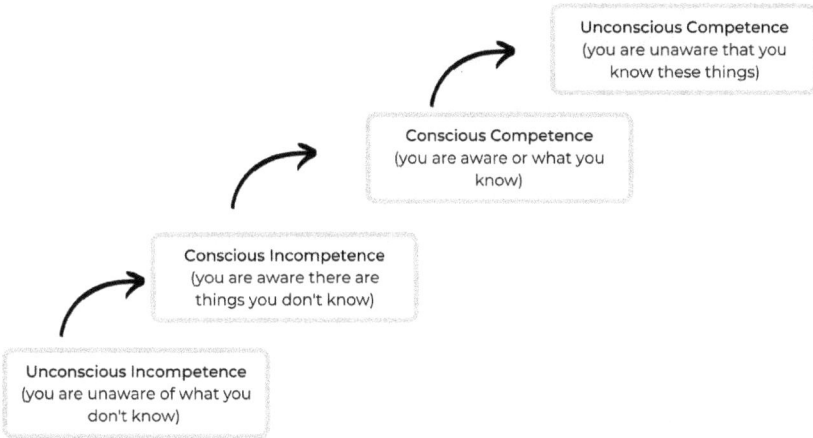

The Conscious Competence Model is a way for us to understand the stages that need to be passed in order to gain a new competence. Competence works on three levels, the individual competencies, team competencies (combined) Organisational competency (overall competency)

Competency is often applied to the individual but can just as easily be applied to an organisation (and to the people within an organisation that combine to form the whole).

There are four stages of competence from 'no idea', to 'all the idea'. It starts with the unconscious incompetence stage and then passes through conscious incompetence and conscious competence until finally getting to the stage of complete competence, what you're aiming for - unconscious competence.

Of course, the path isn't always linear. Sometimes the stages have to be moved through several times before the ultimate end goal is reached.

Unconscious Competence

The first stage of the matrix is unconscious competence. In this stage, the learner is completely unaware of their incompetence. In fact, they may not even be aware of the competence itself (either that it exists or that it's important to them) or even of the skills that underlie that competence.

In terms of the organisation as a whole, this could be a marketing or compliance gap – something it doesn't even realise is missing from its competencies until its performance is impacted. Of course, in order to start developing, the learner (in this case, the organisation) must first recognise that it needs that skill. And the best way to do this is through an organisational development process.

Conscious Incompetence

In this second stage, there is an awareness of what's unknown or Conscious Incompetence (sometimes referred to as the Johari window). A leader, team or organisation knows what it doesn't know, and understands that it needs this skill in order to compete better within the market.

Once leader, team or organisation becomes aware of a gap in competencies or a weakness in an area, it must make a commitment to do what it takes to gain those skills – whether that's through upskilling its workforce, implementing a new system or something else altogether. As the leader, it's your job to lead the organisation through this process. Recognise where the gaps are, and look to recruit, retrain or upskill to fill the competency gaps.

Conscious Competence

Over time, and with commitment, your organisation will move into the next stage – Conscious Competence. At this stage the organisation has gained the competencies it needed and has implemented the processes and people to ensure that it happens across the organisation as a whole. But it's not seamless or smooth yet. It still takes concentration, updating and fiddling on the part of the employees that oversee the skill or competency. In other words, it isn't automatically built into the fabric of the organisation yet.

Unconscious Competence

The last stage is Unconscious Competence. It's at this level that an individual would have developed it enough that it would be a second-nature ability. Within an organisation, a suite of skills becomes an Unconscious Competence when it is seamlessly integrated into the foundational processes of the organisation as a whole. At this stage it can be performed in tandem with other vital competencies by skilled staff as part of their standard roles.

Competencies Versus Skills

Until now, we've been using the term competency more or less interchangeably with skills. But, in fact, they are not really the same thing. Competencies aren't skills precisely – instead, they're the umbrella over all the skills, knowledge, information and more that a person needs to do their job, or an organisation needs to reach its organisational goals. So, in fact, one competency could be made up of many different skills.

The Conscious Competence Model is an excellent method for developing organisational-level competencies, especially where an organisation needs to backfill gaps. But how is this done at a more granular level?

The Organisational Development Process

The organisational development process is an integral part of the Conscious Competence Model. It is this process that allows an organisation to begin to move through the states of the model and develop superior competencies.

You can think of the organisational development process as much like the personal development process, but at the organisational level. It's a research plus action process that helps an organisation to understand its problems, set goals and implement changes. When an organisation goes through this process, it sets itself up to make significant improvements in its own overall performance. And it can track these changes with measurable results.

The Organisational Development Process Cycle

The organisational development process cycle is used to help identify areas where development could or should be pursued within an organisation. While this should certainly be used to develop competencies within the organisation as a whole, it can also be used to make improvements or manage any problem or challenge that a business faces. The broad steps help an organisation to make changes quickly and problem solve efficiently.

Steps

1. Identify the problem. Look to reports, employees, systems that gather data and more, to find and identify problems that need to be rectified or gaps in competencies.
2. Assess the situation. The next step is to make a formal assessment of the problem that's been identified. Review the documentation, interview and survey stakeholders, hold focus

groups or otherwise find a way to gather all the facts so you can develop a solution.

3. Create an action plan. Next take your solution and create a plan to put it into action. This might mean implementing some training or bringing in different staff with required skills, for example.

4. Monitor and report. As soon as you implement your plan, start gathering data and monitoring results. It's important that you understand whether or not your solution is actually creating the development that you're looking for within the organisation.

5. Repeat. If the process didn't give you the results that you were looking for, repeat it, find a new solution and re-evaluate. Continue this until you have a solution that gives you the competency you need within the organisation.

In order to get the most out of this process, the entire organisation needs to be involved. That includes helping to identify the problems that exist and working towards a solution. Ideas should be sought out from all levels within the organisation, and all employees encouraged to contribute.

By utilising this process your organisation will be able to identify those problems that it isn't currently managing (or managing well), as well as those skills and learnings that are currently lacking.

Playbook for Leaders

After developing your competencies at the organisation level you'll want to set up your playbook for leaders. This is the set of guidelines and templates that will help each leader within your organisation to develop their own role and team competencies. It maps out the skills that lie beneath the umbrella of each competency and helps the leader to determine what needs to be done to take their team to a superior level on that particular competency.

At this stage, your competencies also need to be rolled out to the managers and employees organisation wide. They need to become part of the culture of the company – an automatic and inevitable piece of its foundation. You can accomplish this roll out via many different routes – highly structured or more organic. But you need to ensure that they're introduced, developed and then reviewed.

Competencies in the Hiring Process

According to SHRM, competency-based selection is 'probably the most common interview style for Fortune 500 companies today'.[70] This method gives the best results for the organisation as a whole, and many high-performing organisations in all industries are choosing this over more traditional hiring approaches.

It's important to remember that just as competencies and skills are different, the job description is different as well. A job description lists the outcomes, responsibilities and tasks that a job requires. On the other hand, competencies are the abilities that are needed to achieve the things on the job description.

With competency-based selection leaders are able to get beyond a potential candidate's paper credentials and measure if the person has the competencies that are needed for specific roles. Research shows that when this type of selection process is implemented, turnover rates decrease to between 15 and 20%.[71]

---

70   Katz, Lee Michael. 'Competencies Hold the Key to Better Hiring'. SHRM. 29 January 2015. Accessed at https://www.shrm.org/hr-today/news/hr-magazine/Pages/0315-competencies-hiring.aspx.

71   Ibid.

Why Does This Matter?

A company's core competencies are essentially what it does BEST. And its organisational competencies describe how it expects what it does to be accomplished. But why do they matter?

Competencies are the framework that organisations use to help focus the behaviour of employees on the things that are the most important within the organisation, and the things that it sees as vital to its own success.

Benefits

The benefits of implementing competencies within your organisation shouldn't be underestimated.

- They provide a common way to select and develop talent.
- They provide an action-focused methodology for demonstrating the values that are key to the organisation's success.
- They provide the standards of excellence for the roles within the organisation, as well as for the organisation as a whole.
- They help distinguish the organisation's products from its competitors.
- They help to create and develop new goods and services.
- They help to decide the future of the organisation.
- They give way to innovations.

It's clear that there are a great many reasons why competencies should be a foundational element of your organisation. But one of the most important is driving the future of the organisation through strategy.

The Competency Theory of Strategy

The core competency theory of strategy is simply the actions that organisations take to achieve a competitive advantage in the marketplace. The concept underpinning this theory is that organisations will have the most success when they orient their strengths to tap into these core competencies.

Let's take the example of the Walt Disney Corporation. Its core competencies are i's ability to animate (particularly in a time when this was an emerging technology), design and tell compelling stories. By focusing on these skills – and creating such iconic animated films such as Sleeping Beauty, Cinderella, Snow White, Fantasia and much more, they built a business model that not only complemented and built on those competencies but opened up opportunities that stemmed from them.

Today the Walt Disney Corporation has a streaming channel with thousands of animated and live action films and shows, multiple theme parks worldwide, a huge array of branded products for sale across hundreds of industries and more. Utilising the core competency theory of strategy allowed them to develop a framework where they could identify their core strengths and strategise accordingly.

Essential Leadership Competencies

Of course, to lead a competent organisation, you will need to develop your own essential leadership competencies. Focusing on leadership competencies and skill development promotes better leadership[72] in the same way that focusing on competencies within an organisation

---

72   Mumford, T., Campion, M., & Morgeson, F. (2007). The leadership skills strataplex: Leadership skill requirements across organizational levels. The Leadership Quarterly, 18, 154-166. Accessed at https://journals.aom.org/doi/abs/10.5465/ambpp.2003.13792974.

promotes better results. In fact, research shows that developing successful leaders is a competitive advantage for multinational organisations[73], in particular, because they face such a variety of challenges.

In today's world, however, it may not matter whether you're working in a large multinational or a smaller, local organisation. The world is moving quickly, and we need to be prepared for fast moving changes, whether they come in the form of a pandemic, or something else entirely.

Research on successful leaders shows that they tend to have a common set of leadership competencies. These include:

- Open-minded and flexible in thought and tactics
- Able to deal with complexity
- Resilient, resourceful, optimistic and energetic
- Honesty and integrity
- Stable personal life
- Value-added technical or business skills[74]

Using these leadership competencies to support your leadership development, will give you the abilities you need to lead your own organisation successfully through the development of its own competencies.

---

73   Caligiui, P. (2006). Developing global leaders. Human Resource Management Review, 16, 219-228. Accessed at https://psycnet.apa.org/record/2006-07786-012.

74   McCall, M., & Hollenbeck, G. (2002). Developing global executives: The lessons of international experience. Boston, MA: Harvard Business School Publishing. Accessed at https://www.shrm.org/resourcesandtools/hr-topics/behavioral-competencies/leadership-and-navigation/pages/leadershipcompetencies.aspx.

Flexing Your Competence Muscle

When it comes to building competence within your organisation, it both starts and ends with you as a leader. As we've seen, your own leadership competencies give you the abilities you need to lead your organisation through change. More than that, your team will also see those abilities, and want to follow you through their own development and that of the organisation as a whole.

Importantly, understanding how to build core competencies within your organisation will guide its strategy and business results. It will help to provide important growth and future proof and sustain your competitive advantage. Being able to lead effectively through the gaining of these competencies is a big part of being a courageous leader™.

Chapter 11

Community

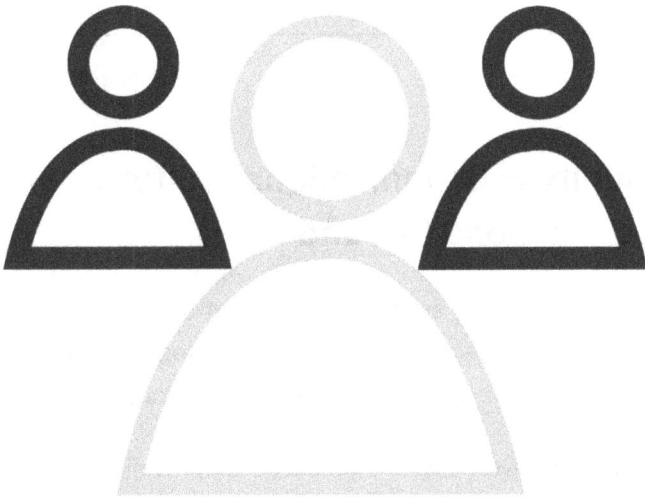

Made For More Definition: To create an atmosphere of trust and respect amongst the team members for cohesiveness and sense of belongingness while embracing conflicts for a healthy outcome.

''Create the kind of workplace and company culture that will attract great talent. If you hire brilliant people, they will make work feel more like play.''

—Unknown

Community is Organisational Culture – How Things Get Done (around here)

Organisational culture is simple to define, but complex to determine. It is how things get done in your organisation. And because of that it is both the 'how' and the 'why' undermining all your decisions and actions.

Many leaders believe culture is achieved by providing perks like ping pong tables, team happy hours or a dog-friendly office. They think that nap-pods or flexible working hours are the backbone of a good company culture that leads to high performance. While these perks can certainly be a great morale boost in any organisation, they are not 'company culture'.

But sadly, many leaders hang their hats on these 'perks' believing that they are the lynchpin that will fix culture issues, drive performance and attract talent. But true culture is driven by internal values and organisational strategy, rather than shiny objects. This includes policies, communication, engagement and employee treatment – each of which drives your organisational culture forward and defines how your employees, and your organisation as a whole, behaves.

This is why culture matters.

Organisations with a great culture encourage innovation, creativity, and growth.

What is a High-Performance Culture?

High-performing cultures impact all parts of your organisation, including engagement, productivity and work quality. Importantly, when you have a strong culture, you are better able to attract and retain top talent.

A Columbia University study shows that job turnover at an organisation with a strong company culture is only 13.9%. On the other hand, in organisations with poor culture, turnover was a huge 48.4% This is why culture matters.

What is a High-Performance Culture?

A high-performance culture is a set of behaviours that drives an organisation to achieve optimum results. Aligning these behaviours with organisational goals, customer needs and employee priorities, creates the positioning for the organisation to reach its desired outcomes, including financial results and retaining and engaging employees.

But to create a high-performance culture, you need to create a courageous culture.

How to create a High-performance Culture

It's no surprise that leaders want to have a high-performing team, rarely does someone pine for a mediocre team. One of the keys to a high-performing team is to establish a common understanding of what high-performance looks like, sounds, like, feels like, and how you as a team measure that.

Ask any high-performing team what their measure of success is, and you will likely hear answers like "increase market share by 10 percent" or "reduce costs by 15 percent."

Ask the same question about their highest priority cultural goals, and you're likely to hear a broad range of platitudes with few if any, numbers. However, high-performing cultures are often characterised by aligning, executing, renewing common objectives, and failing forward. This way, teams with the same definition of culture understand the specifics that matter to them and the right tools to measure those specifics.

Integrating culture change efforts with business improvement initiatives is often a bottom-up approach, whereas culture affects all aspects of an organisation and needs that holistic approach.

Few employees have too little to do. This means that culture change efforts running as stand-alone programs typically are last on the list and rarely succeed. Successful efforts need be fully integrated into your core business initiative. Meaning culture becomes everyone's responsibility.

How to create a High-performance Culture

Establish a common understanding of culture and community, what are you trying to create, and have metrics for it.

Ask any high performing team in any company what their highest priority business goals are, and you will likely hear answers like 'increase market share by 10 percent' or 'reduce costs by 15 percent.' Ask the same question about their highest priority cultural goals and you're likely to hear a broad range of platitudes with few, if any, numbers. However, high-performing cultures are characterised by an ability to align, execute, and renew common objectives. This way, teams with the same definition of culture understand the specifics that matter to them, and the right tools to measure those specifics.

Integrate culture change efforts with business improvement initiatives

Few employees have too little to do. This means that culture change efforts running as stand-alone programs typically are last on the list and rarely succeed. Successful efforts should be fully integrated into your core business initiative.

Courageous Organisational Culture

Winston Churchill once said. 'Courage is rightly esteemed the first of human qualities, because... it is the quality which guarantees all others.

Much like its counterpart in humans, organisational culture is a vital part of every successful organisation. And that is for precisely the reason that Winston Churchill posits – it's the element that guarantees all the strengths and excellence of your organisation that will follow.

Having a courageous culture allows you to take an innovative and future-looking course, forge new ground, react and manage inevitable disruptions and shocks and, of course, engage in courageous conversations.

Of course, courage in an organisation, especially one that becomes endemic enough as to become the central element of the culture, needs to first be found in the organisation's leadership. This is especially important in times of extreme disruption and change – times that we're currently facing right now and will likely face much more of in the future.

Change and disruption lead to uncertainty, anxiety and fear. And when any entity – whether an individual or an organisation – are afraid, they tend to look inward with a goal of protecting what they've got, rather than looking outward, with a drive to innovate or advance. But these are also the times when courageous entities who bravely look outwards and forwards can reap big rewards.

So as courageous leaders how can we support our organisations to become courageous? How can we build up this competitive advantage, particularly in times of change?

The answer is by creating a courageous culture.

Creating Courageous Cultures™

What is a Courageous Culture™

Courageous culture™ is one where the set of behaviours within an organisation supports members of that organisation to not only feel safe to take risks, but also gives them reason and guidance to do just that.

How Do Organisations Create Cultures™

Organisations who want to create courageous cultures do so by implementing five steps or cultural elements.

Create a feeling of psychological safety

Courageous cultures start with courageous leaders, but all cultures will fall apart without the support of courageous employees. And the first step in helping to have courageous employees is to work with them to identify and adopt positive qualities and behaviours that will bolster them through uncertainty and change. This starts with building psychological safety.

When employees have a feeling of psychological safety, they believe that they won't be punished, embarrassed or humiliated for asking questions, or speaking up with ideas or concerns, or even when pointing out errors. They feel safe to do their jobs well, and with an eye to making the entire organisation better.

When employees feel psychologically safe in the workplace, they feel free to be themselves, and to offer their full minds to their work. They are better able to see areas for improvement, for innovation, for development and are comfortable laying themselves on the line to achieve those things. That is courage.

Refocus on possibility, not probability

Too often as leaders we focus on the events that are most likely to happen next – the ones that lie directly ahead of our organisation's current path. But when you focus there – straight along your current trajectory – then you're working from a place of probability rather than a place of possibility.

Instead, you need to have the courage to shift your point of view beyond the limited horizon and strategise about the things that could be possible in the future. You need to have the courage to look five, 10 or even 20 years into the future, so you can move beyond the small margins of improvement found in probability to the leaps that can be found in possibility.

And when you can do that, you can inspire that courage in your employees and your organisation as well.

Inspire curiosity and inquiry

We're often rewarded for having 'the right answer' to questions or 'the right solution' to a problem. That's how we've been taught since childhood, and it has likely been reinforced by organisations we've been part of since then.

The problem with this approach is that instead of fostering a culture of curiosity and inquisitiveness, you're creating one of competition, where your best and brightest employees are jockeying to give the one and only 'right' answer. A courageous culture cannot be a competitive culture. It needs to be one that is open to all ideas, that fosters questioning, collaboration and interest in others' ideas.

It's in the sharing of this open perspective that idea-generation flourishes, and future innovations and high performance grows.

Explain 'why'

As human beings we are wired for purpose. We're built to be inspired by the 'why'. Partly that's because we want to understand that the way we use our time and energy, and the end results we're striving for mean something. While that 'something' doesn't necessarily have to be world alerting, most of us do need to feel that we're doing more than just earning a paycheck.

Feeling inspired is vital for courageous employees, and that means that it's vital to creating a courageous culture. Giving the members of your organisation the context (the 'why') around the what and the how is especially important during times of change because it helps everyone understand the larger considerations that are driving strategies and decisions, allowing buy in. The more information your employees have, the more they understand why they are being asked to do what they do, the more engaged they become and the more resilient they are to change. And that gives them the capacity for courage.

Challenge Your Employees

Many of us live in our comfort zones – the space where familiarity and routine give us a sense of predictability and, therefore, safety. When it comes to our employees (and this argument could apply to every area of our lives) being in a career comfort zone is the antithesis to building a courageous culture. When you're in your career comfort zone, you know pretty much everything there is to know about what you're doing. You understand every aspect of your job. And you aren't challenged at all.

Employees who are in this position – who aren't facing challenges – have no opportunity to grow or become more courageous (or, more importantly, to create a *habit* of courage). But challenging employees to push out of their comfort zones and grab new opportunities and new challenges is an act of bravery in and of itself.

When it comes to challenging the employees of your organisation, the place you're trying to reach is one of 'productive discomfort'. This is the optimal level where an individual is uncomfortable enough to feel challenged but not so uncomfortable that they are unproductive. Experts believe that this optimal level is achieved when employees reach a place where they are required to uplevel their skills or capabilities and embrace a new level of anxiety (for a short time) eventually leading to an expanded comfort zone.

Be clear on the culture you want within your team.

In the same way that you shape and communicate a vision, you also need to spell out the culture you are striving for.

Can you describe the culture of your team and your organisation? If you were onboarding a new staff member, can you define the culture of your team, what's important, what are the defined behaviours and norms? More importantly, can your team describe what aspects make up the culture of your team?

If not, you can discuss which aspect of the current culture are we happy? Which aspects are we unhappy with?
What do we need to do more of?
What do we need to do less of?
Does everyone agree to these behaviours?
What will we do to celebrate? What will we do if we go off track?
How do we measure this?

Connect to the Bigger Picture

It's more than likely if you're reading this that at some stage throughout your leadership journey you've passed a posted on the wall that outlined the vision, mission and values of the organisation you worked for.

What you perhaps haven't talked about with your team yet how important it is for employees to be a part of that compelling future. For targets to be meaningful and effective in motivating employees, they must be tied to larger organisational ambitions when staff don't understand how the importance of their roles, and how they fit into the overall organisation success, the more likely they are to become disengaged.

A few years ago, I was working with a local council who were going through a culture change, I was working with the library team, and they mentioned they weren't really that important in the scheme of things. However, what we did when we worked together was identify how very important their role was to the culture and overall purpose of the Council. In many cases a library is the most public facing aspect of a council. They were able to navigate people to find the information they required. Being able to reframe their understanding of the importance of their role in the overall organisation gave a sense of purpose and improved employee engagement.

Employees want to be a part of a compelling future. They want to know what is most important at work. And, most importantly, they want to know what excellence looks like. Understanding the bigger picture helps them to see those targets, and for them to be meaningful and effective. On the other hand, employees who don't understand the bigger picture, or the roles they play within that picture, are more likely to become disengaged.

Take Time to Celebrate

In this busy day and age, we often set our sights on the next thing to achieve. It's important to remember to celebrate along the way. Celebrate the milestones once they have been reached, celebrate the small achievements along the way. Taking the time to celebrate is important, it acknowledges everyone's hard work, it creates time to spend together as a team, it boosts morale, and keeps the momentum going. It's important to take the time to recognise achievement and how instrumental each person has been to the success.

Employee Empowerment

As a leader, your employees will trust in your decisions to positively impact them. But at times they expect to feel empowered to make those important decisions that are directly or indirectly related to them. The most successful leaders work towards enabling employees to reach their full potential. Here's how you can foster growth among them:

How to create a High-performance Culture

Establish a common understanding of culture and community, what are you trying to create, and have metrics for it.

Ask any high performing team in any company what their highest priority business goals are, and you will likely hear answers like 'increase market share by 10 percent' or 'reduce costs by 15 percent.' Ask the same question about their highest priority cultural goals and you're likely to hear a broad range of platitudes with few, if any, numbers. However, high-performing cultures are characterised by an ability to align, execute, and renew common objectives. This way, teams with the same definition of culture understand the specifics that matter to them, and the right tools to measure those specifics.

Integrate culture change efforts with business improvement initiatives

Few employees have too little to do. This means that culture change efforts running as stand-alone programs typically are last on the list and rarely succeed. Successful efforts should be fully integrated into your core business initiative.

Spell Out Your Preferred Culture

In the same way that leaders shape and communicate a vision, they also spell out a picture of the culture they are striving for. This can often be just a set of guiding principles or values, but the best seems to go further by establishing preferred behaviours that support these values: Which aspects of our current culture are we happy/unhappy with? What preferred behaviours do we need to create the culture we want? What behaviours actually get rewarded round here? Which unacceptable behaviours are actually tolerated here? How do we measure up against each of our preferred behaviours?

Internal Communication

Internal communication needs to be on the top of the agenda – Have they heard the message? Do they believe it? Do they know what it means? Have they interpreted it for themselves, and have they internalised it? Organisations that encourage open communication in the workplace are often characterised by a vibrant atmosphere. There should be a fluid line of communication with an unbiased and open conversation no matter the topic of discussion. Make sure the flow of information is smooth from the top level to the entry-level employee.

Employee Empowerment

As a leader, your employees will trust in your decisions to positively impact them. But at times they expect to feel empowered to make those important decisions that are directly or indirectly related to them. The most successful leaders work towards enabling employees to reach their full potential. Here's how you can foster growth among them:

- Show them your trust
- Provide the required training

- Communicate the vision clearly
- Don't avoid small talk
- Allow freedom within the limit

Developing Your High-Performing Team in Your Courageous Culture

Your team will become better, more productive, more engaged and more high-performing when you implement the values and elements of a courageous culture. But just because you have those elements in place, doesn't mean you can now just sit back and rest on your previous hard work. In order to have a high-performing and courageous team operating in a courageous culture you need to continue that development.

Set metrics and implement tools

Continuing the development of your courageous high-performing team begins with building in a process for setting and measuring metrics around culture goals. These goals need to be built around the ability to align and execute common culture objectives and include implementing the right tools to measure their success.

It's important that these culture change efforts are in line with business improvement or innovation initiatives. And that when you measure them, that you are measuring how well your culture is working to help drive those improvements or innovations forward. They must be measurable because few employees have too little to do, especially those high performers. Successful efforts should be fully integrated into your core business initiative so that these high performers can see how their culture focus is playing out in real terms.

Set Healthy Stretch Targets

Stretching your employees outside of their comfort zones is an important part of setting your courageous culture within your organisation. But once you have it set up, it's not a set and forget – it must remain an important focus going forward.

Setting Healthy Stretch Targets

Employees tend to rise to the standard set for them. The more you expect, the more they will achieve. But there is a fine line between healthy stretch targets, which can energise an organisation, and bad ones, which can dampen morale

Continue to expect your employees to rise to the standards you set for them. The more you expect, the more they will achieve.

So, continue to energise your team and the entire organisation will benefit.

Creating strong internal communication

Going forward with a courageous team in a courageous culture, you need to continually focus on your internal communication. In fact, it needs to be on the top of the agenda.

Always ask yourself, 'Have they heard the message?' And if they have, then, 'Do they believe the message? Do they understand it? Have they internalised it?'

You need to ask these questions continually in order to encourage open communication in the workplace. There needs to be a fluid line of communication. You need to allow for an unbiased and open conversation no matter the topic. And you need to ensure that information flows smoothly from the top level down. Again, this is especially important in times of change and disruption in order to keep your courageous culture looking forward rather than becoming mired in the drama of the moment.

Celebrate milestones

Celebrating milestones might sound like the kind of thing you'd read about in a glossy magazine or on an influencer's social platform, but in fact, it's an important part of your continuing approach to a courageous culture. When you and your team reach a milestone, celebrate. Acknowledge your team's

hard work. This boosts morale and keeps up the momentum especially in times when courage could wane (due to shocks to the business or external disruptions).

Collect feedback

Your courageous culture must be a feedback-rich culture. Feedback is part and parcel to having the kind of open culture that courage needs.

Ensure that you are always collecting feedback from your employees and teams. But, additionally, ensure that you're accepting of any feedback that might come your way at any time. Transparent feedback is vital to helping you keep your finger on the culture of your organisation and will shed light on how your employees themselves are feeling about your culture and if there is anything that needs improving. Knowing that you are supporting your employees in the right way will ensure that you're achieving the results that you are looking for in terms of your organisation's culture.

Flexing Your Organisational Culture Muscle

Creating a courageous culture is vital to the success of your organisation, and to the high performance of your teams. But building in that essential set of behaviours that creates a courageous culture does take commitment both now and into the future. If you're just relying on ping pong tables and nap pods, you won't truly be impacting on your organisation's culture at all.

But if you do put in the time and the energy to create a courageous organisational culture, you'll find that your organisation is stronger and more future focused. And you'll find that your teams and employees have increased engagement, productivity, work quality and outcomes.

Chapter 12

Lead With Impact

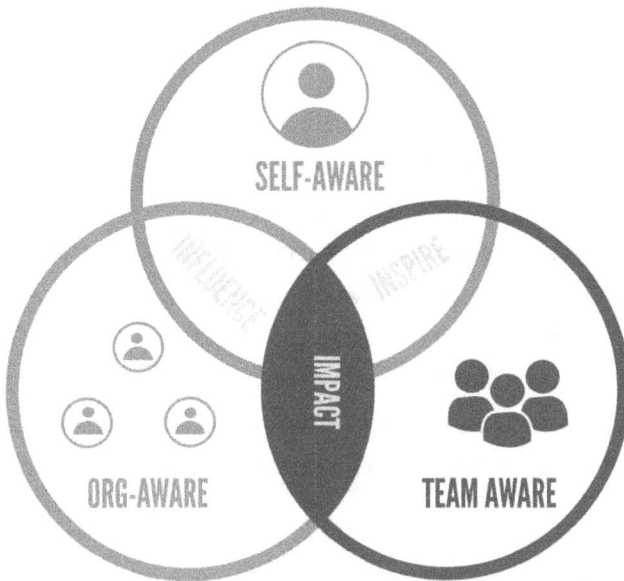

Made for More definition: High-impact leadership is making long-lasting, positive contributions in the lives of people, organisations, communities and even the world. working with team and organisation for impact to clients, customers and stakeholders. They're project orientated, but not necessarily the best communicators or motivators.

"Leadership is about making others better as a result of your presence and making sure that impact lasts in your absence."

—Unknown

There are very few people – and even fewer leaders – in the world who would be unaware of Steve Jobs today. He is well-known as one of the most extraordinary leaders, as he successfully led Apple to become the most valuable company in the world in 2010. He is often described as a visionary and genius, and people who knew him saw that he also had an uncanny ability to capture the essence and value of other people's thoughts, ideas and creations. In other words, he didn't just capture his own brilliance, but others as well, harnessing them for the good of Apple as a whole.

Today, it's been almost ten years since his death. Yet Jobs is still one of the most important elements of Apple's success. Why? Because Jobs led with lasting impact. His visions, values and leadership are still part of the Apple organisation today.

When you're gone from this planet, what will people remember of you? Steve Jobs' impact on Apple, and frankly the world, even today is a powerful reminder: leaving a legacy, lives through people. Your results matter, of course. But they can often be forgotten. When you connect, develop and inspire people, when your positive impact has been integrated into the lives of those you touched, and the organisations you worked with, your legacy will ripple far beyond your tenure.

Leading With Impact + Courageous Leaders™

Leading with impact begins with courageous leaders. When we work with leaders and organisations to build better leaders and teach the art of courageous conversations, then we can make and create change makers. Those change makers are vital today because, whether we like it or not, change is upon us. And as always, it is happening at the speed of light compelling us to new and better ways to create lasting impact in this changing world.

As leaders, we have a huge responsibility to the people that we lead and it's vital that we're aware of the impact that we have. This impact is not limited to what happens in that nine to five period where we are actually operating within our organisation. It also includes what's happening outside of the traditional workplace as well.

We all know very well the flow on or waterfall effect of what happens outside of the office – whether it's economic upset, a pandemic or even our employees' personal lives. So, if you're a leader of people, you must make sure that you are having a significant impact not only our own personal lives, but also on the way that our business is growing and succeeding. And, of course, we must continually strive to understand how that growth and success is being driven by our impact on our most valuable organisational asset – our people.

Courageous leaders who lead with impact will always be contributing positive interactions and impacts on their people who will then turn around and take that home to their families and the bigger world.

Build a High-Performance Organisation

When I was early in my leadership journey, I was handed the keys to open an office in the CBD and recruit my own. It was a fantastic experience. I was young and driven, and I built my team up of other young and driven professionals who were a lot like me.

We became an extremely high-performing team because we had that high-performing culture. We all became quite good friends, and that meant that we never wanted to let each other down. We worked hard, and we pulled together, and our team won award after award. And some of that – not all of it of course, but some of that – came from the leadership impact that I had in building up this high-performance culture.

And of course, now at Made for More, we're building our own team of high performers because excellence is one of our core values as well. So, it's important to me that, as a business, we work with leaders and organisations to help them get the best performance out of their people, and perhaps even out of leaders themselves. And a vital part of this is leading with impact.

Generating Energy

As a leader, it's sometimes difficult to always be the one motivating all those around you, including yourself. Sometimes you can feel your energy begin to wane.

Brendon Burchard, in his book *High Performance Habits: How Extraordinary People Become That Way*, lists six high performance habits. One of these is focused around generating energy. Burchard's theory is that high performers have developed the ability to keep their own energy high, while still expending it to lift the interest and stamina of those around them. And it is this ability that leads to sustained performance and growth within a team and organisation.

For myself, with four children and a busy practice, I often have to work to keep my energy high. I do tend to be someone that takes on and can handle quite a bit. But I do get overwhelmed at times. So, one thing that I do to protect and grow my energy is meditation. When I find that my own energy is waning, or if I get a little bit in a manic cycle, I know that it's time to stop, drop and meditate allowing myself that space to focus on and rebuild my own energy for the next steps.

It might not be meditation for you but maintaining your energy in some way is vital if you want to lead your team with impact over the long term.

Driving the Culture Bus

We've talked in great detail in the previous chapters about the culture of an organisation, but it's important to reiterate here – as impactful leaders, it's our job to make sure that we are driving this culture bus. That begins with your own modelling, and steps through all the elements that drive culture, including any culture change efforts.

Culture must be something that leaders are continually focusing on and thinking about. Successful efforts should also be fully integrated into your core business initiatives. And it's vital to ensure that any decisions that you're making for a team or organisation are fully aligned with the culture that you either have, or that culture you're working to create.

In the same way that leaders shape and communicate a vision, they also spell out the picture of culture they are striving for. This will be a set of guiding principles or values, of course. But the most impactful leaders seem to go further by establishing preferred behaviours that support these values.

Setting Stretch Goals

Leading with impact also means leading your team to growth and success. But growth and success won't appear if you and your team continue to operate solely within an already well-trodden path. Instead, we need to be setting healthy stretch targets for ourselves and also for our staff and teams.

People tend to rise to the standard set for them and the more that you expect, the more that they will achieve. But there is a fine line between healthy stretch targets which can energise a team and an individual, and the ones that are simply too far to reach, or demand too much energy. These simply end up lowering morale.

In terms of stretch goals, we must continually connect to that bigger picture – the culture bus, if you will. We need employees that want to be part of that compelling future, who want to know what is important at work and what excellence looks like.

Imagine you're rolling out a project over the next 90 days, but you've got an element that needs to happen this month. 90 days may be too long for some teams to focus (and for many teams it might not), but a single month may be highly doable. Point the arrow at this first target and drive towards that first success. Once you've got there, it will be far easier to motivate your team to move towards the next target. That is impactful leadership.

Communicate with Clarity

If you want to lead with impact, you need to ensure that your message is being delivered in the right way to the right people. Most of us will be familiar with the concept of Chinese whispers. And this kind of communication can and will happen within the organisational setting if you're not careful to override it with strong communication directly from you as the leader.

The second part of this is to ensure that the message that you're communicating is actually being heard. While we may believe that we're being really clear and specific with what we're saying, perhaps that's only clear and specific to us. The message being received by our people can sometimes be quite different to what we were expressing or expecting. So, it's vital to ensure that as a leader what you're saying is actually what people are hearing.

Celebrate the Everyday Wins

At Made for More one of the things that we do as a team is celebrate our everyday wins. In fact, every Friday we spend a couple of hours celebrating the things that we've accomplished that week. If you want to lead with impact, it's imperative that you celebrate the 'impact' – not necessarily *your* impact, though you want to celebrate that as well, but the impact of each member of your team and of your team within your organisation. Understanding your own impact will drive your energy. And when your team understands their impact, it drives their energy as well.

Sometimes in business, we are very forward focused, and we can get caught up in all of the things that need to get moving and happening. But celebrating the everyday wins allows you to take the time to look back and see those tiny steps that are moving you towards your goals. These wins (and the accompanying celebration) also become part of and builds out your high-performance culture as well because people are driven to have a reason to celebrate each Friday. For me, often on a Thursday I might think, "Oh, what am I going to celebrate on Friday? I'd better do something awesome today!"

Team Empowerment and Letting Go

Celebrating your everyday wins is one way to empower your teams. And if you've been leading teams for a while (especially if you've been leading them with impact), you'll know that team empowerment is the secret sauce to business and leadership. When you get really good at this impact, empowering your staff, it's also code for letting go.

Letting go of some or your own responsibility and giving it over to other people can be very difficult. If you have your own business, you may be used to wearing all the hats. Giving a part of your little baby away can be really tricky. But when we start empowering the people around us, it gives us the space to move from the little picture to the big picture. When you have less things on your plate, you have more mental clarity to be the best at the things that you are still focusing on within your business or organisation.

If you want to start letting go, begin by thinking about the things that are not in your genius zone, or that you're perhaps good at but don't like doing. Start looking for those skills within your team or look to bring them in when you're building your team.

When it comes to employee empowerment, as a leader, your staff must be able to trust that your decisions are taken to positively impact them and the entire organisation. But they also must feel empowered to make the decisions that are within their scope of work. Creating the space for your staff to do this enables them to reach their full potential, fostering growth and further success. Beyond that, this shows them that you trust them, and that they can trust you.

Leaving a Lasting Legacy

When you are an impactful leader, you *will* leave a lasting legacy. It may not be one that ranks in the billions of dollars or have a worldwide impact like Steve Jobs, but it will still be lasting and important.

If you want to be an impactful leader with a lasting impact, consider the following:

Prioritise People Over Results

Results are important. But impactful leaders understand that results are driven by people. The market may still care about your results three years from now, but your team won't. They won't remember whether you hit all of your benchmarks. But they will remember how you led them during that time. And that will highly impact any future performances as well.

To prioritise people over results, start paying attention to how you speak to or communicate with your team. Do you always focus on the results? When you talk about wins are these numbers based or goals based, or are they broader than that? Do they take in other factors? You want your focus to be on the human being, not just on the 'human-doing'.

Invest Resources in Your Team

Investing in your team's professional growth is an important part of being an impactful leader. Whether that's online courses, conferences or semi-regular internal workshops taught by external experts, your team will have more success and make a bigger impact in the future with professional development. It will also serve to carry your legacy even further.

Ask your team to propose areas they would like to develop. This could be business development, writing skills, tech training and more. To have the most impact, concentrate on areas where you can see the skills leading to a win for them, as well as the organisation.

Connect in Person

'Leadership by email' is risky if you want to be a high-impact leader. Email is not a conversation, it's a serial monologue. Sometimes it's a necessity and communicating virtually can be fine for quick notes, replies and disseminating information. But it won't create the

 lasting impact or build the kind of strong, trusting relationship that drives engagement and performance. That simply won't be sustained by a barrage of emails.

Instead, make an effort to connect over the phone as well as in person. Have regular office hours and be visible within the office space so people feel free to reach out to you in a more casual, organic way. Holding regular one-on-one meetings is another great way to connect, as is having offsite team building activities. Your legacy will endure through your positive human interactions.

Model The Behaviour You Want

Your team is watching you, and they often learn more about behaviours from observation than from listening to you. Don't just spend time parroting the behaviours you want in your team. Integrate them into your work life. Make them a part of your own impactful leadership. Then invite your team to attend meetings and participate in calls so they can see these behaviours in action with senior leaders, customers or other stakeholders.

Of course, employees won't emulate all leaders. You must be a leader that has engendered their loyalty and trust – one that they *want* to imitate because they admire you or what you're accomplishing. If you are an impactful leader who has built (and continues to build) good relationships with your team, who empowers them and gives them opportunities for growth and who models the good behaviours you want to see, then you're in a good place to earn that loyalty and trust.

The Waterfall Effect In Leadership

It takes a lot to become a leader. Take a ballet performance, for example. The Sydney Dance Company has 16 dancers at any one time and during a performance. Each will be part of the corps, soloists or principal dancers, and each has a specific role to play. But it is the energy, focus and specialisation of each dancer that combines to produce the beautiful outcome. The principal dancer might be the centrepiece, but it's the dancers in the corps that give the depth and grandeur to the performance as a whole.

Let's look at the above scenario in terms of an organisation. Imagine an organisation where leaders optimise time and potential to the fullest. This would be a situation where each member of the team is valued for what they can do individually and for what they bring to the whole. This leads to a cascading effect within the organisation known as the 'waterfall effect'.

The waterfall effect is an idea originated from Paul H. Burton's book, *The Waterfall Effect: Six Principles for Productive Leadership*. It is simply the idea that leaders, 'who spend time focusing on the right goals, engaging in the right activities, and connecting with the right people produce the waterfall effect of "cascading' success'".

For Burton, the waterfall effect demonstrates the process whereby benefits from 'focusing on the right goals, engaging in the right activities, and connecting with the right people' flow through a team, then an organisation, into the customer or client base and finally out into the community or even the world – in other words, impactful leadership (Steve Jobs and Apple are a good example of this). In his book, Burton sets out the six leadership principles that can help a leader become an impactful leader capable of cascading success.

Developing field vision

Field vision is a leader's ability to take in and respond to numerous data feeds. These are inputs from senior leaders, from financial documents, from external events and much more. The ability to assimilate all this information and make sense of it is one reason why many corporations prefer to hire mathematicians and engineers in leadership positions even in companies that have nothing to do with those fields. It's not the knowledge per se, but the ability of being able to process large data quickly that is so desirable. This essential skill saves the organisation time and money and contributes towards the waterfall effect.

Keeping the glass half full

Keeping the glass half full refers to the impact of positive attitudes from leaders. When you have a positive workplace, it allows employees to ideate, experiment, innovate and create. But this doesn't happen in a vacuum. A positive workplace needs an optimistic leader who see the world as a glass half full. This energises and motivates the entire workforce and helps to produce a waterfall effect of success.

Leveraging the value of silence

The ability to be silent is an important skill for an impactful leader in all cases. It allows you to carefully consider your responses to your team, colleagues and senior management. It helps you to embrace holding back communication when the time isn't right. And it allows you to develop the important skill of listening.

In other words, a visionary leader knows when to stay quiet. Silence is a highly useful tool for impactful leaders that can produce great results.

Peeling back the onion

Onions have layers and peeling back an onion is quite an apt metaphor for uncovering the hidden potential in others. As an impactful leader it's your job to help your employees to peel back those layers by believing in their potential and taking action to help develop it. This is professional development of course, but also opportunities to provide other and ongoing support, providing leadership opportunities leaders and simply being aware of their skills so you can utilise them at their best and boost employees' performances.

Setting the bar

As an impactful leader you set the bar, and, as we've already discussed, you need to set the bar higher than your team can currently jump. Establishing these 'stretch' expectations (much like stretch goals) is a vital part of creating waterfalls of success within your organisation because it turns consistent but average performers into high performers. Of course, harbouring unreasonable expectations is a recipe for disaster as this both demotivates your team and impacts on their performance.

Triaging priorities

Triage in the workplace doesn't necessarily mean putting out fires. Instead, triaging priorities refers to the constant review and determination of what needs the most urgent attention at that time. Of course, what needs the most urgent attention might not be a problem per se. It might instead be an opportunity – such as a chance to upskill employees, or the merger with a competitor. However, understanding where you need to focus your attention most urgently is a vital element of the waterfall effect that highlights the importance of prioritising action.

Impactful leaders must be able to constantly juggle responsibilities and opportunities and understand what needs to be prioritised and what does not.

Flexing Your Impactful Leadership Muscle

An impactful leader can create a huge difference in a team and organisation. If you've ever worked with a leader who wasn't very effective (or impactful) then you recognise that poor leadership comes at a cost, particularly to employees who can feel demotivated, demoralised, unproductive and unsupported. And all of this will certainly affect business outcomes.

On the other hand, impactful leadership drives waterfalls of success. It creates opportunities for employee and team growth, drives productivity and ultimately leaves organisations with the highly desired high-performance culture.

Conclusion

How to Continue Your Courageous Leader Journey

CAPABILITY

CLARITY

SELF AWARE

CONFIDENCE

COMMUNITY

COMMUNICATION

COURAGEOUS LEADER

ORG AWARE

TEAM AWARE

COMPETENCE

CURIOSITY

CHANGE

COMPASSION

As the saying goes 'A rising tide lifts all boats'. We need to be looking at creating mentally healthy workplaces, managing change, cultivating trust within teams and across teams, open honest communication, and as we know–Good leadership comes from the top.

What we're going to be seeing more of:

- More ASK than Tell
- Time to grieve – similar to when we saw travel cancelled and people started were in shock, we're going to see that period of grief.
- Employee led work.
- Empathetic leaders – wellbeing has been at the front of mind for leaders.

If you feel that your team needs Courageous Leaders™, let's have a chat about our leadership training packages, seminar presentations, coaching and mentoring programs and a way to fast track your team for 2021.

Speaking

If you're looking for an engaging, enthusiastic and a (little bit) funny speaker to inspire, educate and fire up the audience of your next event, team offsite or conference, go no further. Specialising in leadership, communication and change, Ally will tailor the session to your objectives, audience and timeframe.

Brining in an external speaker can really lift engagement and add another level of variety and perspective at your event.

Learning

Courageous Leaders Intensive

Small amount of time but massive impact. This one week intensive and immersive program will have your leaders walk in on a Monday, and out on a Friday with a completely different mindset, an overflowing toolbox of tools, and enough motivation and momentum to keep them going for the next 12-36 months.

Courageous Leaders™ Program

Our flagship program is designed to take leaders from frozen, frazzled and flat out to clear, confident and courageous.

Courageous Conversations™ Masterclass

Courageous Speaking™ Workshop

Designed for leaders and teams who are looking build their confidence in speaking, whether it's presenting at a meeting, an all-staff session, or presenting to board.

Courageous Teams™

Dose of Courage™

Short bite sized pieces of leadership inspiration and impact. A tailored approach consisting of individual two-three hours sessions that can be run virtually of face to face.

:

Made For More Academy™

Self-paced online learning to take your remote work to the next level.

Executive Coaching and Mentoring

Lead with Courage™

CEO Advisory Boardroom™

Specifically designed for C-suite and executive, a mentoring and networking program to have Ally in your back pocket for when you need a sounding board, bounce ideas off of, a little bit of cheer squad and a whole bunch of support.

Madeformore.com.au/CEOAB

Stay Connected

Resources

Download our Courageous Leaders Audit, whitepapers and other resources read to read, share and amplify your leadership.

https://www.madeformore.com.au/resources

Read

Blog – https://www.madeformore.com.au/blog

Listen

Podcast

Love some inspiration in your ears. **The Made For More** podcast will keep you up to date with leadership experts from around the globe. Ally interview leads, business owners and experts in the field. Available on Apple Podcast, Android, and Spotify. Madeformore.com.au/podcast

Radio Show

Overwhelm to Owning it in an international radio show for leaders in business and organisations who are looking for tactical tangible advise.

Madeformore.com.au/radio

Watch

Prefer visual learning, extend your thinking through short videos to take your leadership to that next level.

Madeformore.com.au/video

About the Author

Ally Nitschke is a leadership expert and Courageous conversation specialist.

Obsessed with all things courage, not he brave kind, the kind that when things feel icky, you do it anyway. Courage where you lean into discomfort. The *'knees weak, arms spaghetti'* kind of courage

Ally helps leaders to navigate the complexities of leadership to accelerate change and have a massive positive impact on work life.

A multi award winning business owner, and recipient of the Professional Speakers Association – Kerrie Narin Scholarship and with nearly 20 years' experience, Ally has helps thousands of leaders develop their leadership vision, confidence and capability. She typically speaks at conferences, runs workshops and programs, consults, coaches and mentors.

She helps HRD's, People & Culture Executive, C Suite, Executives and Transformation and Change leaders build the practical foundations for connection, compassionate and courageous leadership. Get out of the hamster wheel and lead to inspire, lead to influence and lead to have a massive impact.

Among her many awards:

- Kerrie Nairn Scholarship 2022 (professional Speakers Association
- 40Under40 nominee
- 3-time award winner for time and productivity
- #5 leadership podcast in Australia
- SA/NT Young achiever of the year

Ally's clients include: (alphabetical)

ActivOT, BHP, Comunet, Dept Education, DHS, JP Media, Harris RE, KWP, LGAs, Ozminerals, National Pharmacies, RAA, RSPCA, SA Health, SA Power Networks, Telethon Kids Institute, University of Adelaide, University of Queensland, Valo, Women Leaders Institute to name a few.

Her clients describe her as modern, fresh, uplifting, very engaging, spectacular, and interesting.

Find Ally Online

Website

www.madeformore.com.au

LinkedIn

https://www.linkedin.com/in/coach-leadership

Facebook

https://www.facebook.com/ally.madeformore

Instagram

https://www.instagram.com/ally.madeformore

Email

ally@madeformore.com.au

Work with Ally Nitschke

To book Ally as your speaker visit www.madeformore.com.au/speaking

For executive coaching visit www.madeformore.com.au/programs

Training programs and events visit www.madeformore.com.au

Rise of the Courageous Leader - Bonus Resources

https://madeformore.com.au/rise-resources

Complimentary Resources:

- Daily Dose of Courage

https://www.madeformore.com/daily-dose

- Complimentary webcast

https://www.madeformore.com.au/events

www.ingramcontent.com/pod-product-compliance
Lightning Source LLC
Chambersburg PA
CBHW071156210326
41597CB00016B/1572